THE IRISHMAN WHO RAN FOR ENGLAND

JIM HOGAN

CURRACH
PRESS

First published in 2008 by
CURRACH PRESS
55A Spruce Avenue, Stillorgan Industrial Park, Blackrock, County Dublin
www.currach.ie

1 3 5 4 2

Cover by Bluett
Origination by Currach Press
Printed by ColourBooks, Baldoyle Industrial Estate, Dublin 13
ISBN: 978-1-85607-958-7
The author has asserted his moral rights.

To the Memory of My Wife Mary

Acknowledgements

I would like to acknowledge the help and support of my brother and sisters and their families in many different ways, especially since the death of my wife Mary. Particular thanks are due to my sister Margaret. I am also grateful to Ron Clarke for allowing me to reproduce 'A Runner and His Wife' from Ron Clarke and Norman Harris, *The Lonely Breed* (London: Pelham Books, 1967).

An Irishman won a gold medal when the European Championships wound up yesterday, but he was the wrong one, so to speak. Jim Hogan, the improbable Irishman, carried the colours of his adopted country to a resounding success in the marathon. It was the ultimate in irony.

Tom Cryan, the Irish Independent, *September 1966*
(from PJ Browne, 'Hogan's Run', Athletics Weekly, 15 June 2006)

Contents

David Bedford

Preface by David Bedford

David Bedford was born in London on 30 December 1949. He was Britain's most colourful athlete of the 1970s. He is now director of the London Marathon.

I set a world record in the 10,000 metres in 1973 and three British records over three different distances, but my career never included a medal at any major track championship. That is why it gives me great satisfaction to write about Jim Hogan, a man after my own heart when it came to training and racing. I would include myself, Hogan and Ron Clarke in the same category. We had many similarities and Jim will agree with me on this. Ron Clarke was my hero and Jim would say the same. I competed against Clarke a couple of times near the end of his career and he was too good for me.

Jimmy was the only one of us three to medal at a major athletics championship. Clarky broke seventeen world records. I broke one. Ron had an awful amount of bad luck. The year he was winning everything the Olympics were at altitude in Mexico. If they had been anywhere else he would have won the 5000 metres and 10,000 metres easily.

I was at the top for four years before I got a leg injury. On a bad day I was sixth in the Olympics and on a good one I broke the world record. I feel happy with my career.

I know that Jimmy has no regrets about his career either. He overcame enormous odds and antipathy but he prevailed. Had he come to Britain a half-dozen years earlier there is no telling what he might have achieved. Bikila was considered unbeatable in the marathon, and that may well be the case, but a fully-fit Hogan in his prime would have given him a rare old tussle.

Jim and myself came from a different era. I'm not saying we were more talented. Talent alone is never enough. I trained three times a day, 200 miles a week. I don't see that commitment in Britain or Ireland any more. Jimmy would get up to 150 at times but he was smarter than I was; hence his longevity.

He was so motivated and so well trained for the European Championships in Budapest (1966) that no athlete could have lived with him that evening, and I mean no athlete. He was driven like never before. Sad to say he had no one to push him, and he won in a hack, as he'd say himself.

You had to be a bit mad to train like we did. I'd prefer to call us characters. Even as a kid I always liked a character! The fact that the first one I ever met was Jim Hogan confirmed this. I knew he was an Irishman, a Great Britain international and famous for running barefoot. He was a crazy character too, in a non-crazy way. If he didn't like you he told you so in no uncertain terms!

Here is an outstanding memory, and people find it hard to believe that this actually happened. Middlesex Championships, Feltham, in the mid-1960s. Hogan is running in the three miles. I'm sixteen. He takes the lead as he invariably did, but he gets totally arsed when no one else will take the pace. He slows, the field slows.

He shouts, he swears and they ignore him.

He stops and walks. They walk. Talk about a Mr Bean moment! He steps off the track and they continue. After a few moments he gets back on the track and starts again. He goes on to win that race and is then disqualified. What a memory. You could not make this stuff up.

As I got older we got to know each other better and Jim took me under his wing. He was good friends with my coach Bob Parker.

At nineteen, I raced at the White City in the AAA Championships and beat all the good senior guys, including Jimmy Alder, a Geordie with a chip on both shoulders. To be fair to him he was a bricklayer and thought all southern athletes were on the soft side, pansies.

He came up to me after the race and said something to me which I interpreted as less than supportive – difficult to understand foreign languages! It was within earshot of Hogan and he had no trouble in understanding the comment. Needless to say, he came to the rescue: 'Leave the boy alone or I'll kill you, Alder.' I walked away, feeling quite good after that.

We started training together, especially on Sundays, when we did long runs of up to twenty miles. These were easy low-intensity efforts unless some bloke started getting restless and wanted to push the pace. We'd soon sort him out. There was one priceless incident that we still joke about. One Sunday, while running through Twickenham, we turned sharply right into a park, then left up a small bank. Jim did not see the sign with park opening hours and kept running at a good clip. He head-butted the sign and knocked himself out. It was as if he had been hit with a plank. He was out cold. Three minutes later he came round, got to his feet and dusted himself off. He denied he had been knocked out and just continued running. I hate to use a cliché, but they really don't make them like that any more.

We have remained good friends ever since those days and we keep in touch. Not only is he a character, he's a gentleman and a good friend. I look forward to having him over at the London Marathon every year.

He does liven things up a bit and somewhere along the way he learned how to sing. I'm not sure about his talent in this field but I wouldn't argue with him about it. In truth he loves the crack and the dancing and he is just as energetic as he was in the old days.

It's a real pleasure to be asked to write this, and I look forward to reading his life story. I know there are still stories that I have never heard.

One last observation: the one thing I always said about Jim is that if the swear-words were taken out he would be a mute. With Jim, though, they are not swear-words, just adjectives! Like I said at the beginning, the man is still a character. His place in the world of athletics is secure beyond doubt. He was a world-class athlete.

Prologue

Writing my story has been a daunting task. The biggest difficulty was what to include because there are so many people, events, memories – enough to fill several books. My one regret is that my wife Mary is not alive because she would have been much better at this. She would have ensured that the relevant details went into it. Furthermore, she had a good understanding of people. Mary was well educated and widely read and would have enjoyed playing an active part in the writing of the story. She was an anchor in my life, even though we were complete opposites. We complemented each other in a way most people would never understand. I keep a picture of her in my car because I feel she is still with me.

It's been a long journey from when I was born and almost didn't live, and from my early training with Mick Potter around Bruree House. Mick was an early influence and then I started to beat him. Without his support I might not have stayed in the sport. I won several races in Ireland, and every Munster and national title with the exception of the four-mile championship. I was never able to win that one.

The move to England opened up a new world to me and I thrived there after settling in. It was a rocky journey at times and not without controversy. I have included much of the controversy in this story. Athletics allowed me to travel the world and visit cities I would never otherwise have seen.

Through the years several articles and stories have been written about me. I have at least four complete scrapbooks dealing with my races, my victories, my defeats. Every now and again an athletics magazine would want to know about my training schedules and plans. Most of what was written about me was favourable, I have to say.

There was only one fellow who wrote for a newspaper in Dublin who always had it in for me. I'd say he hated me, and I don't really know why. Maybe because he was a Dubliner and I came from down the country. I think my declaring for Britain didn't sit too well with that bloke. It's all water under the bridge now. What he wrote didn't bother me then and never did after. I'll tell you one thing: I had no liking for him either.

But there's a couple of pieces that Mary and I were happy with. The first one was written by a Bruff man – I'd say a good ten years ago – and later reproduced in other magazines or websites.

The other piece is one of my out-and-out favourites. The fellow who wrote it, Paul Howard, showed up in the yard one day, cool as you like. I thought he was lost. He was wearing glasses and looked like a teenager. I knew some bloke was coming down from Dublin to interview me but sweet Jesus, when I saw your man I had to laugh. He couldn't have come at a worse time.

A nephew and I were drawing bales of hay, taking advantage of the good weather. It was warm that day. Your man didn't have a clue about farming or any of that, but I didn't have the heart to tell him to go away. As I found out, he probably wouldn't have listened to me anyway.

So we get to talking easy enough and it went well. He was on top of his game and understood a bit about athletics. Boxing, I think he said, was more to his liking. We had a great few hours together and the guy was cute enough to let me ramble on and on. Before he left he promised me he would do a good feature because the material was what he wanted.

Well, that young fellow was true to his word. Jesus I got a shock the day I read it. He had me pegged the whole way. I'd say it's easily one of the best features ever written about me. Mary liked it, but said it would have been better if he had left out the bad language. Sure there was no harm in it.

I often wondered what became of him. He told me he'd keep in touch and come back again but that's easier said than done. He was a bright young fellow and it was only lately I found out that he had done very well for himself as a writer. I'd say he made nothing at all writing about athletics. Now I hear he's a bestseller and I'm chuffed for him. More luck to him; he was a smashin' young fellow and I hope he makes a fortune.

Almost Big in Japan

In Tokyo in 1964, Limerickman Jim Hogan spent most of the marathon on the shoulder of the legendary Abebe Bikila. But with three miles left, and a silver medal assured, he quit, exhausted. When his moment of glory finally arrived at the European championships two years later, he was wearing a British vest.

He fetches two chairs from the kitchen, sets them down in the yard and tells you to sit as comfortably as the hard surface will allow, because Jim Hogan's life story is long, lads, make no mistake about it, it's long. Jaysus it is. It's long and hectic and angry and inspiring and expletive-filled and wonderful. He wants to tell you about the marathon in Tokyo, how he ran the race for a laugh and found himself in second place at the turning point in Chofu City, not a word of a lie, the only runner in the race who could still see Abebe Bikila eating up the road in front of him. And he wants to explain how near to death he felt when he gave up the race three miles short of the finishing line with an Olympic silver medal there for him, if he could only stay on his feet.

He wants to tell you all this but he's a busy man. That trailer-load of hay bales, they're not going to shift themselves, lads, and Jaysus Christ he can't be frittering away sunny afternoons like this one inside in the kitchen supping tea and raking over the past. Yet the memories keep coming back unbidden and soon he is telling his stories again, with the same breathless energy with which he ran.

The splenetic spirit that raged in Jim Hogan as a young man still burns strongly at sixty-seven. Those blazer-wearing bastards in the Irish Athletics Association: he wants to tell you all about them. How he ended up running for Britain just to spite them; how, on the proudest day of his life, when he won the marathon at the 1966 European Championships, it was 'God save The Queen' that he stood to and the Union Jack that was raised. He doesn't regret it for a minute.

And remind him to tell you by the way that his name isn't Jim Hogan at all. Or rather it wasn't. It was Jim Cregan. But that's a story in itself. And those bales of hay, he'd want to be making a start on them soon before it starts getting dark. But still there's so much to say.

Paul Howard, 'The Greatest Olympic Stories Never Told,'
The Sunday Tribune, *23 July 2000.*

Jim Hogan – A Rare Breed

'I feared no opponent. If you're looking around you at the start of a race worrying about them, you'll win fuck-all.'

The year 1964 was the most turbulent in the history of Irish athletics since the 1930s. The International Cross-Country Championship was held in Leopardstown Racecourse on 21 March. The race was a low-key affair. Irish television offered a paltry £400 pounds to carry a live telecast, an offer that was turned down. Francisco Aritmendi of Spain, a twenty-five-year old sports groundsman, won the race in front of a modest crowd. Athletics fans elsewhere had to make do with a radio commentary. Jim Hogan took fifth for Ireland and the Irish team was sixth out of nine. Great Britain won the team event.

It was a race that Hogan might easily have won. He explains: 'I had trouble getting over the obstacles, and lost about five seconds over each. Each time I made up ground on the Spaniard, only to fall back on the obstacles. Normally I would have run him into the ground.'

In the 1966 European Championships, Hogan would win the gold medal in the marathon in an English vest, the summit of his turbulent athletic career. What follows is a glimpse of Hogan's accomplished career. Mary, his beloved wife, succumbed to Parkinson's disease before Christmas 2001.

Only two good things came out of Ireland in the 1960s – Arkle and Jim Hogan. This was a sentiment that Jim Hogan used to hear around Chiswick, and he smiles as he recalls it. Although a little embarrassed by the hyperbole, Hogan is pleased to be linked with the great chaser. That the sentiment embraces the two dominant passions of his life – athletics and horses – is tacitly acknowledged.

7/215131D

'I have always loved the horses,' he says. 'Arkle was marvellous, and I saw him win all his races in England.' Hogan is a mere five pounds heavier, at nine stone seven pounds, than he was at the peak of his running career. He was light enough to be a jockey, and spent many of his early years riding out for Joe Hogan, patriarch of the Hogan racing dynasty in County Limerick.

Jim Hogan and his wife Mary returned to Ireland in November 1995. 'Mary wanted a bit more space, and I was glad to come back,' he says quietly. To see him workout in Bruff sports field, one would think that little has changed. He runs barefooted, his distinctive gait moving lightly through the strides. Two to three miles per day is his limit but, characteristically, there's a hint of quality about them.

It was on this field, newly opened in 1956, that Hogan won one of his five Munster titles at the four-mile distance. 'I set out the track,' says Ronnie Long of Bord Lúthchleas Éireann. Local pranksters had scattered boxfuls of thumb-tacks all over the place. After winning his race, Hogan discovered that he had run the entire distance with a tack embedded in the sole of his foot.

It would take a lot more than a thumb-tack to impede Hogan's rapid progression to stardom.

Hogan began his athletic career quietly and furtively in his native Athlacca, five miles from Bruff, in County Limerick. 'If you were seen running in those days, people thought you were mad,' he says. 'You'd have to steal out.' His parents didn't know about his running until his name appeared in the *Limerick Leader* after he had come second in the senior county cross-country race. 'After that I cut a track on our own field with the scythe. My sister Betty had an alarm and a clock for timing me. People wouldn't believe the hardship we went through.'

When he was twenty-six, Hogan went to England. 'I should

have gone four years earlier,' he says, 'and I would have made the Rome Olympics. It would have given me experience for Tokyo.' He didn't run for about six months, having had difficulty finding suitable employment. He worked at various jobs until he found the ideal situation as a groundsman with Brentford and Chiswick local council.

His running needs were accommodated: he was allowed to take time off work to travel and compete. It took him about a year to establish his dominance with the Polytechnic Harriers, 'and then for about eight years nobody could get near me.' He thrived in the organised training and support of club running.

Success brought acclaim and international recognition: 'In 1960 I came back to Ireland and ran as Jim Cregan. I was under the impression that you wouldn't be allowed to run in England if it was known that you were an NACA runner. So when I was there I changed my name to Hogan. A lot of people don't understand it. Hogan was the first name that came to mind, and had no significance whatsoever.'

Notwithstanding the mystery surrounding his name, there was no ambiguity when it was time to compete. Jim Hogan was selected to run for Ireland in the 1964 Olympics.

Extract from an article by PJ Browne in LetsRun.com. (2003),
based on an earlier article in the Irish Examiner *(1998)*

1

My Early Life

I was born – Jim Cregan – in Croom hospital on 28 May 1933. I was very sick as a baby so my mother had to leave me in hospital for six weeks. When she went to bring me home I was still not very well. About a mile from home she had the feeling that I had died so when she got home she left me in an outhouse. A friend who was at the house went outside to see me and realised that I was still alive. He said that one day I would be famous.

I have seven sisters and one brother. Two live in the United States, Nora and Frances; there are two in England, Margaret and Josie. Mary lives in Ardpatrick and Tess is back in Boherard Cross, Athlacca. Betty is living in Mayo now, after living in England for years. Mickey Joe is in the home place in Athlacca.

When I started out running in 1952, Betty used to come out and time my runs with an old wind-up clock. I was doing 400 yards and 800 yards and she helped me quite a bit. My brother, Mickey Joe, never did any running at all. I'm pleased to note that they are all in good health and keeping well. Mary is the eldest and I am the second eldest. My father died in 1976 and my mother died in 1984. They both lived into their eighties and may the Lord have mercy on their souls.

They had tough lives, and that's putting it mildly. Like all small farmers, they worked hard all their lives. It was very difficult to make a living in the 1940s and 1950s. My father and I used to cut a lot of hay for other people. We had three horses – there was no machinery then – and we cut for all the local farmers.

We'd often be out at three in the morning with the three horses. At lunchtime we'd change horses to keep them a bit rested and up to the work. 'Twas hard work, I'm telling you, but sure we were all in the same situation; all the people of the area had to work just as hard. A small farmer might be all right in the summer with fifteen or so cows, but in the winter there was no money coming in. The main thing was to try to make enough money in the summer in order to see you through the winter. There would be winters where it was tight enough.

You can well imagine how my mother and father felt about my running. It just wasn't done; you'd be considered an oddity by neighbours and they'd be talking about you. I can't say I blame them for that. If the situation was different I'd have been laughing with them at the clown tearing around the place.

Of course all that changed dramatically when I won a national title. That must have given me some credibility and might have justified the madness. All I can say now is that thereafter I wasn't as self-conscious about the training. I suppose winning a title made the running acceptable.

TRALEE 1954

I began at cross-country in January or February of 1952. I was fourth in the County Limerick novices championship, then I was second in the junior and second again in the senior, so I was improving all the time. I didn't go beyond county-championship class until the track season. I started on the track in July 1952, and I'm talking now about a track pegged out on grass, not the high-tech jobs you see today.

By the end of the year I had won an Irish championship in Tralee: the five miles – in twenty-six minutes dead. That was actually an Irish record then. I was nineteen. You could say that was my first significant breakthrough in Ireland.

It was a very special day for me because my father made the journey specially to see me run. He enjoyed my win; it was one of the proudest days for him watching me win that title. That title was more meaningful for him than my winning the gold medal in the European Championships. You see that was something that could be talked about locally, an All-Ireland Championship. That would have impressed the local boys and there was great pride in being a national champion.

My father didn't see me compete a whole lot, which is understandable. First of all, getting to a track event or championships wasn't easy. Then there was the work on the farm to consider. There was always work and more work and taking a day off had to be planned well in advance. My sister Margaret came to a good few meetings with me and at one of them she won the ladies' cycle race.

My best day in Ireland was in Tralee in 1954, at the 'Kerry Day Out Sports'.

The feature races on that day's programme were the Five-Mile Championship of Ireland and the Three-Mile Championship of Munster. Hot favourite for the Irish event that afternoon was the holder Mick Joe Cleary from County Tipperary. According to the *Limerick Leader*: 'The barefooted Cregan ran Cleary and the rest of the opposition ragged on that occasion. Less than an hour later Cregan was back for the Three-Mile Championship of Munster race and won easily. In the aftermath of that race Mick Joe Cleary came over to Jim Cregan and said, "Cregan, you're a horse of a man."'

It was also the first time I raced against Tom O'Riordan. During my career I won twelve Irish championships in all, eleven southern Irish championships and eighteen county championships.

Later on, I was delighted that my mother and father were able to come up to Santry to see me run the Irish six-mile championship. My brother Mickey Joe accompanied them. I'm glad to say that I ran well again, even though conditions were very windy and cold. I lapped a very good field of Irish athletes, including Bertie Messitt, so it was good occasion for all of us. By this time I was working and training in England.

If I had stayed in Ireland (as an athlete) I would have wound up with nothing. I'd have achieved nothing, just reached a certain level of competence and packed it in, as many lads did.

Pa McAuliffe is one athlete who comes to mind. He was a talented runner over the 400- and 800 yard-distances, but he retired young. He was twenty-three when he gave it up, a bit early I thought, but it does prove the point I just made about the benefits for me of leaving the country. When I started running in 1952, there was hardly anyone doing it. But we had a good club in Croom and there were also some very good runners in the Cappamore area – Paddy Carmody, Willie Daly.

We wasted a lot of time running in Ireland under the NACA (National Athletic and Cycling Association). The officials were no help because you couldn't run outside the country. But the one good thing about the NACA was that you had athletics every Sunday from May to September.. You could go somewhere almost every Sunday and race, whereas under the AAU (Amateur Athletic Union) you didn't get as much competition except in Dublin.

I still find it remarkable that we were able to run the distances we ran. I never ran more than four miles in any night's training, and that would include four or five fast quarter-miles. I never actually trained for the distances I ran and I still won ten-mile championship races. I look back now and I think – how did we run it?

I should clear up two areas of confusion here. I went to England in February 1960 to get work, nothing else. Actually I had given up athletics at the time. I hadn't run since August 1959 and didn't start again until April 1960. Another area of confusion is my name. After a while away from Ireland I changed my name to Jim Hogan by deed poll in order to compete in Britain. At that point Jim Cregan's career ended and Jim Hogan's began. From then on I used the name Hogan even when I raced for Ireland, for instance in the

Tokyo Olympics in 1964. I thought this was the only way I could compete outside Ireland but I found out later that it wasn't the case.

There were things that made it easy for me to leave Ireland There were no jobs and the country was riddled with class distinction. I saw more class distinction in Ireland in the 1950s than any other country I've ever been to. And I've travelled more than most, I'd say.

When you came out of church of a Sunday morning, the big farmers would stand around inside the wall. The small farmers and labourers would gather and stand across the street – they never, ever mixed. If you went to a social event and you were nicely dressed, they'd look at you as if to say, 'Why are you here?' I experienced the full brunt of that snobbery in my time but I always had the last laugh, especially at horse events and the like. I knew the owners, the trainers and the jockeys and there was always a warm greeting.

You don't have that snobbery among genuine horse people, no matter what their background. They accept you on your merits and never turn their back on you. Thanks be to God, with more money in the country the days of looking down on a fellow are long gone.

2

Running Barefoot

People have always asked me questions about running barefoot. I know I was the exception, certainly among white runners. With high-technology footwear to suit every surface nowadays, I sometimes wonder if manufacturers haven't gone over the top. I suppose the name of the game today is sales, money and sponsorship. I have no problem with any of the top athletes making as much as they can because they work hard for what they get and it's a relatively short career. You're only an injury away from being totally forgotten about.

I'm not sure of the advantages of running barefoot for anyone except perhaps for myself and a bloke called Bruce Tulloh. So I can't say I'd recommend it. But my times always showed that I could run faster barefoot. One year I ran all my races with spikes on and my times were diabolically slow compared to what I ran barefoot. I'll give examples to show this.

My best barefoot three miles was 13 minutes 19.6 seconds whereas with spikes it was 13 minutes 30 seconds. That eleven-second difference is massive in a track race, like night and day. Over six miles, I ran 27 minutes 35 seconds barefoot, but only 28 minutes 18 seconds with spikes. How can you compare it? When I put spikes on I felt tied to the ground, and when I finished a race, I felt as though I hadn't run as hard as I could. I was fresh as a daisy ten minutes later.

I taped my toes when I ran barefoot. I put on a piece of plaster the day before, so it would fit into the skin, and definitely stay on for three miles, even six miles unless the track was very bad. I had to wear spikes when it was muddy, though. I loved running in the White City, even though many times the track was well chewed up when it came to the middle-distance events and that made racing a bit more of a challenge for all competitors.

I was first and foremost a track runner. Cross-country would have been second on the list for me. I never considered myself a marathon runner. It was a distance I came to late in my career and even though I was successful at it, at heart I was always a trackie, which to my mind is the essence of running.

By and large I was a front-runner. It was often a tremendous strain leading all alone, and I never had any help. I arranged with different blokes for them to run with me but they always backed out when the pressure was on.

More to the point, though, I was conscious of not having a good finish. This meant I had to try and take the finish out of the kickers by taking it out fast and staying there. I don't know why, but I was never able to run faster than sixty-two seconds for the last lap although a runner of my ability should have been able to do sixty.

THE WHITE CITY

The White City was built for the 1908 London Olympics. It was the first of all Olympic stadia to be purpose-built, and at the time it was the largest stadium in the world. Its capacity was 150,000, with 68,000 seated and 17,000 covered. After the Olympics it was used for track and field, greyhound racing and speedway. From 1932–70 it was host to the AAA Championships, before Crystal Palace was built.

The stadium was demolished in 1984 and the site is now home to BBC Radio headquarters in Wood Lane.

The White City was a marvellous place to run, out on its own. I loved running there; it had tradition and history and the atmosphere was special. I never ran a bad race in the White City; I had great success there. The six-mile AAAs was the next best race to the Olympics. The cream of English athletes were there. The odd outsider, like Gamoudi, raced there. The times were always fast.

I broke the Irish record there two or three times. I broke the British 10,000-metre record there; that day it was at least 75°F, very hot. I could always run much better when the weather was hot. I didn't mind the heat at all.

Breaking the British record there is one of my special memories. At four miles I was sixteen seconds inside the record. The last two miles were very hard and I was two seconds inside the record. So you can see the fall-off. Fergus Murray took me through the first eight laps. After that I was on my own, so I was running against the clock, a very big challenge.

The condition of the track was not always the best. I

remember people getting blisters while wearing shoes. In Finland they rolled the track before all the top events. When I first went to England they used to do that at the White City but then they stopped rolling it. This was the case at the AAAs where the race went on after about four hours of competition and no one put a brush to it.

That was terribly unfair on the athletes and it could have been avoided. On the Continent the athletes' needs came first and that's as it should be. I'd get annoyed with the way they watered the track as well. They'd water the track on a Thursday for a Saturday meet but when the sun came down it turned the top inch of the cinder into dust. The right time to water the track would have been the morning of the race.

Even so, I have fond memories of the old stadium. I feel it was a privilege to have been able to compete on that track, and that some of my best performances took place there.

3

MY WIFE MARY

Getting married to Mary was the best thing I ever did in my life. I was introduced to Mary Murphy in February 1961. She was living near Shepherd's Bush at the time. We started going out and in July we came home to Ireland on holidays together. Within a couple of weeks of our return to England we decided to get married. We were married in Chiswick on 8 September 1961. The wedding was a small affair with only four or five people attending.

Unfortunately, Mary was taken ill at the wedding and she had to be rushed into hospital that night. I didn't know it then, but Mary would be plagued for much of our marriage with illness, doctors' visits and hospitals. Teddy Ryan, my best man (he introduced me to Mary) and myself stayed at the hospital for most of the night. We went home to get a little sleep, and the next morning I went back to the hospital and spent an hour with Mary. It was not the start to married life that any couple would want. Then I had to go to work.

Mary assured me that she was okay and told me to get on with things. That would have been her attitude during our time together: keep going, don't complain and look on the bright side of things. I'm amazed that she was able to stay

Jim with his wife Mary in their Chiswick flat.

positive because I can tell you that woman suffered.

Getting on with it applied to athletics as well. There was nothing I could do for Mary while she was in the hospital except to visit her every day. I ran with Polytechnic Harriers and we were due to take on a very good Mitchum team in the 4x1-mile relay in Hurlington. We matched our weakest runner with theirs and I decided beforehand to take the last leg – my best time in the mile was an unremarkable 4 minutes 20 seconds. The Mitchum boys were good with a couple of 4 minutes 9- and 10-second-milers.

It came to the bell and my team had given me a lead of 40 metres, a good head start but leaving me with a lot of work to do. My best chance of getting a result was to go as fast as I could for the first half-mile. I split the half in 2 minutes 3 seconds, and won the race with a time of 4 minutes 15 seconds. Their anchor ran a 4 minutes 13 seconds but we had enough in hand to win the relay. Then it was back to the hospital to see how Mary was getting on. She spent the best part of three weeks in hospital and recovered. They didn't find out what was wrong with her at that stage.

Marrying Mary made a tremendous difference to my life in England, all of it for the good. They say that opposites attract, and that was surely the truth when it came to the two of us. She was definitely the opposite to me in so many ways. Mary was very well educated and always held down a good job; she went from strength to strength as far as jobs were concerned and her dedication to work was brilliant. She never missed a day; she left the house on days I wouldn't have gone. You never knew what she was doing at work; she never brought that home or discussed it.

The great thing about Mary was that she let me get on with my training and never interfered in any way. Needless to say she gave me a stability that I had never had in England up to that point, and this showed in my racing and performances. In 1964, the Olympic year, once again Mary was unwell but she wouldn't hear of me not going to meets and championships. They picked me for Tokyo, and while I was in Tokyo, she had a very serious operation. It was then they found out what was wrong with her. She'd had an operation before ever I met her and they left a fragment of something inside her and that caused all the problems.

I don't blame Mary's illness for what happened to me in Tokyo: that is explained elsewhere. It has to be remembered that athletes are not machines. Things go wrong unexpectedly. We were more prone to injuries than athletes today because the medical know-how in relation to athletic performance was still in its infancy. But it was clean, pure sport – the money wasn't in it to tempt any athlete to cheat. We all toed the line on an equal footing and the best athlete won on the day.

There was only one exception and that was when they ran marathons at altitude. The Africans had an in-built edge there. You could hardly blame them for that, though. They trained hard, and I'd nothing but admiration for them. Unlike the rest of us, many of those fine men went home to poverty, and in some cases jail and physical abuse. They were quiet, shy lads, the Africans, and I loved them. I'd get on forever with them.

LIFE IN ENGLAND

We were very happy in England, the two of us. I loved England. I love it to this day. My biggest thrill is going back to race meetings, meeting old friends, dear friends. England was good to me. I love the English people and they haven't forgotten me.

Mary and I weren't drinkers and avoided the pub scene altogether. Mary'd go to a few race meetings with me, places like Sandown. In the early years, the wrestling matches were a big attraction, and we'd go to a match and have great crack altogether. Mary went to all my home races. She only went abroad once and that was to Belgrade. It wouldn't have been easy for her to get time off from work and she liked to keep her holiday time intact so we could go away together Our movements were limited because we didn't have a car. Then in 1970, Mary's company moved to Feltham, and we moved from Chiswick to a house in Hampton, which was just up the road from where she worked.

One of my regrets was that Mary was not able to accompany me to Buckingham Palace. I was invited there twice, first when I broke the world record and received a plaque from Prince Philip. Then in 1968 the whole team were invited to the Palace after the Olympics. Mary couldn't go; it was strictly for the athletes in those days. She would have been thrilled to go but she was beaming with pride just the same: her husband, a Limerick man, going twice to Buckingham Palace to meet royalty. We had come a long way from the poverty of rural Limerick.

Looking back, I wish I had worked for myself earlier on in

my time there. It was only in the last ten to twelve years that I struck out on my own. I also worked for a bookmaker on the racetrack for six or seven years, and I enjoyed that. Any job I liked I stayed at, but I left several jobs because they didn't suit me. Working for myself gave me a lot of satisfaction. You worked and you got paid. If you're good at your job you get asked back to do others. Anyone who asked me to do a job – be it gardening, landscaping, putting down brick paths or building water fountains – always asked me back. I liked being my own boss, and I wasn't keen to ask for time off from work in order to go away to athletic meetings.

I remember one time when I was working for Pearl Assurance they wouldn't give me a half-day to go and run at the White City. It was 12 July 1963. The boss was a bit of a bastard and I said to him, 'Look, they're all scared of you in here. They wouldn't even come up near your office. But I'll tell you one thing: I walk out and the whole world knows me, or they will after I've run in the White City.' I finished second in the AAA Championships, and I got a phone call from the boss the next day wanting to know would I come back and work for him. But I told him what to do with his job.

4

THE EUROPEAN CHAMPIONSHIPS, BELGRADE, 1962

I started running well on 18 February 1961 when I finished second to Martin Hyman in the English Southern Counties Cross-Country race in Epsom. I won seven races between then and 8 July 1961. Between the day I got married in September 1961 and April 1962, I ran nineteen races and won eighteen of them, a good number of them cross-country and relays. I never stopped winning and I wasn't running at my best at all then. Over the course of the next several months my improvement was massive. I got better and better with each race. That was the beginning of my big breakthrough in England. My confidence and my belief in my ability were reaching new levels.

From April 1962 until the end of that year I ran many of my fastest times. On 2 May I ran a three-mile Irish record in 13 minutes 33.6 seconds at Leytonstone, outside London. Five days later at Paddington I broke another Irish record, the six-mile, in 28 minutes 7.2 seconds.

For the rest of 1962 I was badly injured but I did compete for Ireland in the European Championships in Belgrade. The selectors told me that if I could run fourteen minutes for three

The 3000 metres at Hurlingham on 25 February 1961.
Poor conditions contributed to my slow time of 14 minutes 36 seconds.
Derek Haith (No 218 in photo) won the race.

SPORTS FACTS

by STANLEY BERGIN

Jim Hogan is new athletic hope

A MONG the standards set by the A.A.U. for the European Championships in Belgrade next September is the figure of 29 minutes 40 seconds for 10,000 metres and 28-40 for six miles, which means that Jim Hogan, Limerick-born but now running with Polytechnic Harriers, has staked claim for inclusion in the party named for that trip.

Within recent times Jim has set Irish three and six mile records and only last week-end broke the latter figure by no less than 38.8 seconds when winning the Middlesex title.

His time for six miles, incidentally, was 28-7.2, so he should have no worries about paying a visit to the Continent later in the year.

I understand that he will be invited to compete at Santry in June, but behind all this attention being focussed on our latest athletic "hope" lies a very interesting story.

Back in 1959 when P. Considine won the N.A.C.A. three-mile title at Crumlin, Harry Gorman was second, and listed at number three was J. Cregan (Kilmallock).

Not so long ago either the name J. Cregan figured on a London team which competed in an N.A.C.A. cross-country race in Carlow.

What is significant is that J. Cregan and J. Hogan are (or were) one and the same person.

Now, I understand, that having gone to England some years back, Cregan changed his name by deed poll to Hogan, under which name he had been competing in A.A.U. events, so that there is nothing, we believe, to prevent him representing this country at Belgrade.

Officials of both bodies were not so taken by surprise as one might imagine when the position was put to them yesterday.

One N.A.C.A. official stated that he had been aware of the dual personality for some time but had not been in a position to press the matter and on the other side of the "fence", efforts were made successfully

A view of Hogan's brilliant

A 1961 article by Stanley Bergin in the Evening Standard.

Another Record For Jim Hogan

Limerick Runner, In Bare Feet, Has Fine Win In London

JIM HOGAN (Poly H.), the 28-year-old Limerick-born distance runner, put up the second fastest world six mile time this year when he ran in bare feet to win the Middlesex County Six Miles Championship in 28 mins, 7.2 secs. at Paddington, London, last night.

Only Basil Heatley (Coventry Godiva M.), the world ten mile record holder, with four-tenths of a second faster, has a better six mile time this year.

Hogan, who is bidding for a place in the Irish team for this year's European championships, beat by 38.8 secs. the All-Ireland record for this distance set up by Bertie Messitt in 1959. He was 1 min. 6.2 secs. inside the county record and this great run followed on to the Irish three mile record set up at Leyton last week.

He made all his own pace and lapped the entire field excepting Nat Fisher (Eton Manor A.C.), who finished 400 yards behind in second place with a time of 29 mins, 11 secs. Peter Mellor (Ponders End A.C.) was third in 29 mins. 29 secs.

After the race Hogan said that he was troubled by the stiff, cold breeze and added that he was sure that he could get inside 28 mins. later in the season.

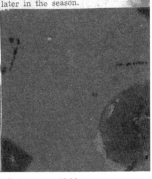

Jim Hogan the barefoot runner, 1962.

miles – a time trial of sorts – they would send me. I was put to the bone to get that time. I clocked 13 minutes 59.06 seconds. I was in a terrible condition. I had a slipped sacroiliac since February without knowing it. I had been running on it and getting away with it until it caught up with me. I was away from work for five weeks. I wasn't fit enough to run but I took the trip because Jack Crump got me a seat on the plane for £20. The Irish paid £10 and my own club, the Polytechnic, the other £10. Mary accompanied me on that trip, and the Irish team joined up with the British team for the cheap flight.

I should not have gone to Belgrade but the money that had been spent on the ticket made the decision easier. Besides, Mary was with me and it was a change of scene for her. I raced in the 5000 metres and 10,000 metres and was forced to drop out of both. The Irish officials were none too pleased with my performance, although they said nothing directly to me. There was one positive aspect to getting injured: I found a man who would take care of me and many other athletes during our careers. I first met Ted Chappel when he was an assistant to a doctor in Wimpole Street in London. Eventually he set up practice on his own. He treated us athletes for nothing. He was brilliant; we'd go to his home and he'd have us right before a race. He never took a bob and never said anything. He was an unsung hero really.

After the European Championships I rested for about six weeks. Fortunately I was treated by Ted Chappel. I got going again in December 1962, winning a seven-mile cross-country championship in Richmond and setting a new record for the course. I finished second in the Irish cross-country

JIM HOGAN from Kilmallock, Co. Limerick is a long distance runner who is seldom lonely, for he is paced by his boss during a practice session at his place of employment, Duke's Meadows Recreation Ground, Chiswick, London. The 30-year-old Irishman, out of work after he threw up an insurance post to compete in the AAA six-mile championship, nipped into the park recently — his daily seven-mile lunchtime run and ran out a groundsman. Now boss Arthur Sainsby, the head groundsman, helps Jim with his training and paces him on his 12 to 15 m.p.h. laps. "Marellous," says Jim. "Open air work, showers on the spot, space to train and they might even be getting a track."

A 1963 newspaper photo, its caption referring to Jim Hogan's dispute with his insurance company boss. The motorcyclist, Arthur Sainsby, was later killed in a road accident

Irish runner Bertie Messitt in a discussion with Jim Hogan, 1963.

Jim Hogan (right) finishes second to Martin Hyman in the 9-mile cross-country race in Epsom, in a time of 44 minutes 33 seconds.

championship in Santry on 23 February 1963. My times continued to improve and on 11 May I broke the Irish three-mile record with 13 minutes 33.2 seconds in Leytonstone, a year after my previous record-breaking success. I then won the British six-mile championship on 3 June at White City. On 12 July 1963 at White City I finished second in the six-mile, breaking the Irish record in 27 minutes 54.2 seconds.

In 1963, things began to fall into place for me and I had a very good year. I continued to run very well and I knew that I would be in top condition in the Olympic year of 1964.

HOPE BEGINS WITH HOGAN

THE Tokyo Olympic Games will be declared open on Saturday, October 10, and will close on Saturday, October 24. The athletics event will be held on the middle eight days, from Wednesday the 14th to Wednesday the 21st, inclusive.

Tokyo is eight hours behind Greenwich Mean Time. The first event, the 100 metres first round, will start at 10 a.m. on Wednesday in Tokyo —3 a.m. here.

Our athletics team to the 1964 Olympics is more representative than our teams in Helsinki, Melbourne or Rome. We will contest the 800 metres, 1,500 metres, 5,000 metres, 10,000 metres, ladies' 400 metres and 800 metres, hammer throw, and possibly the marathon.

We will figure in the first final on Wednesday the 14th at 9 a.m. our time, when Jim Hogan runs in the 10,000 metres. This is, in fact, the first track final of the Olympics and Hogan may well set a high standard for the rest of the team to follow.

When I spoke to the 31-year-old Limerickman in London over the week-end he was very satisfied with his form. This, he said, will be the crowning race of his career and he's done everything possible to ensure that he puts in his best ever performance.

It has been a long difficult road for Hogan from that day 12 years ago when he decided to try his hand at running, to the day when he represents his country in the Olympics. Nineteen was a late age to begin a running career, but he knew from his ability at other sports and from his natural endurance that he could be a distance runner. He had been running for only 2 months when he won his first Irish title, the N.A.C.A. 5 miles championship.

The young farmer from Kilmallock was determined to realise the potential he knew was his. As he said himself, he thought he trained hard then but now he knows that he only played at it. He won numerous honours at home but he wanted to get further afield.

With the dual purpose of improving his running and earning a better living he emigrated to England but the faraway hills were not so green. In 1958 he represented Ireland in the European Championships in Belgrade but, not fully recovered from an illness, he failed badly.

Last year he ran second to Ron Hill in the British A.A.A. 6-mile championship in a best ever time of 27:54.2, which placed him third best in the world for 1963 at this distance behind Ron Clarke of

Australia and Hill of Britain.

This year he got a job as a groundsman with the London Parks Council, which gave him better opportunities for training. He climaxed a rigorous cross-country season by winning the Irish title and coming fifth in the International Championships at Leopardstown in March.

He went to Dublin to run in the Irish 6-mile championship, which he won un-opposed in 28:03.0. Then came his greatest ever 6 miles in the A.A.A. classic at the White City, London, on July 11. He came third in 27:35.0, Bullivant winning in 27:26.6, with Hill second in 27:27.

This time makes him fourth best in the world this year and places him among the favourites for Tokyo. (To get his equivalent time for 10,000 metres, add 60 secs. to his 6-mile time.)

It gives some idea of Hogan's standard when you consider that his time of 28:35 is 42 secs. better than the Olympic winning time of the great Emile Zatopek in 1952, and 1 min. 25 secs. better than Zatopek's winning time of 1948.

According to Hogan, the man to beat at Tokyo will be Australian Ron Clarke, who last week ran 28:36.0 in Sydney and who last year set a phenomenal new world

1964 Irish Press *article by Brendan O'Reilly.*

5

THE TOKYO OLYMPICS, 1964

It was a happy Jim Hogan I spoke to at the Crystal Palace on Saturday. He had just received news of his selection by the Irish Olympic Council in the Irish team for the Tokyo Olympics in October.

'It's a great relief to know at last that I'm on the team,' said the thirty-year-old Limerick man. 'It will be the climax of my running career and I feel sure that I can do justice to my selection.'

His coach Gordon Pirie is very pleased with Hogan's form. 'He could shatter the world 10,000-metres record any day now if he got down to it. But why should he even try? The big target is Tokyo, and we're going to work towards that from now on.'

Brendan O'Reilly, Evening Press, Wednesday, 5 August 1964

Gordon Pirie has long been associated with athletics and even in his busy days of competitive running always found time to lend a helping hand to some unknown athletes in many parts of the world. Jim Hogan has great confidence in Pirie's training schedules and feels not alone that he will have done the necessary amount of work for his Tokyo bid, but that he will have the first-class advice of one who has perhaps the greatest practical knowledge of any coach in the world today.

This will be a great help to Hogan, for he sometimes suffers

Sixteen members of the Irish Olympic team left Dublin Airport yesterday en route to Tokyo. Pictured are, front row (left to right): John Ryan, John Lawlor, Maeve Kyle, Paddy Fitzsimmons and Sean McCaffery. From top down (left): John Hooper, Michael Ryan, John Bouchier-Hayes, Joe Feeney and Sean O'Connor. Right: Basil Clifford, Tom O'Riordan, Derek McCleane, Jim Hogan, Brian Anderson and Jim McCourt.

from lack of confidence, but with a man like Pirie by his side, I think Hogan will be ready to make a bold bid for a medal, especially in the longer 10,000-metres event. His time for the distance certainly puts him in with a great chance, and, even if he gets into the first half-dozen, it would be a magnificent boost to the already growing reputation of Irish distance running.

W.P. Murphy, the Irish Independent, *Wednesday 30 September 1964*

The Olympic marathon in Tokyo wasn't nearly the disaster people said it was but it got a lot of publicity that I didn't want.

I was always willing to listen to good advice from people I respected, be they coaches or athletes. The role that Gordon Pirie [British runner, 1931–91] played in my career has been exaggerated. Yes, of course, I listened to what he had to say, and he was very helpful at one point. But I trained with good athletes and raced against them on an ongoing basis. I think that was more important than any specific coaching.

Two months before the Olympics, I was on holiday in Germany with twenty-five other athletes. The Germans had never seen a relay before so we decided to stage one. There was a bunch of lads from Belgrave Harriers and Blackpool. They formed four teams of six, with each man running a little over two miles. I decided I'd run the whole thing by myself and a few of the athletes thought I was mad. I got away anyway and I covered the full thirteen miles in 61.5 minutes. The relay teams were behind me by over two minutes.

I decided then that I was right for the marathon, although this was the longest run I had ever done in training or competition. I used to be scared that my legs would crack up on the road. I wrote to the Irish officials asking to be put in the marathon. Their reply was no, I was to run the 10,000 metres. It wasn't until I was on the plane to Tokyo that I found out they had in fact entered me also for the marathon. This wasn't good news at all because my training was geared to the track race. I had done no training with the marathon in mind and my longest run was seven or eight miles. I put all marathon thoughts aside because the 10,000 metres was the race I was prepared for and I was expecting to compete well.

Shortly after I arrived in Tokyo, Mary went into hospital once again for a very serious operation. It was then that they found out what was wrong with her. She'd had an operation before ever I met her and they left a piece of something or other inside her and that caused all the problems. I could have stayed with her but she'd have none of it and urged me to go. Now I don't blame Mary's illness for what happened to me in that race.

In the 10,000 metres I was a bit worried. You have to make up your mind before the start: 'Will I go with them or will I hang back.' Sitting in was never my style so I went out with the leaders. I went past the 3000 metres only seconds outside my best time and obviously it was impossible to maintain that pace. After twelve laps (half-way) I got a very bad stitch, something I never had before or since.

The doctor who was treating me for my injury suggested that stress may have induced the stitch. It could also be that I started out too fast. I'll never know really.

Jim Hogan is last in the field in the 10,000 metres at the Tokyo Olympics, October 1964. USA's Billy Mills won gold, Tunisia's Mohamed Gammoudi silver and Australia's Ron Clarke bronze.

It was a disappointing run and when they lapped me I dropped out. I was heavily criticised for quitting and I didn't do justice to the level of preparation and fitness that I had attained. I feel strongly that when a man is lapped in a race, he's just in other people's way. I know when I lapped a bloke and he got in my way I was very annoyed. I know you've got to accept that not every fellow can be a winner but in a big championship race I think lapped runners should be told to move to an outer lane or get off the track altogether.

There were about five or six days between the 10,000 and the marathon. Ron Clarke and myself got together and he said to me, 'Jimmy, we'll have a go at this. There's no pressure. We'll do it for fun, and the outcome doesn't matter.' I wasn't too enthusiastic because my legs were in a terrible condition after the 10,000 metres. But I had run so badly that I agreed to do it, partly out of desperation and wanting to show people that I was no quitter.

I went to see Bikila's coach the day before the marathon. He had a machine for toning muscles; when he laid it on my leg I nearly I nearly jumped off the table. He was a lovely fellow, a Finnish man, and he said to me, 'Your feet are in such bad condition that if you get to six miles you'll be doing very well.' I wasn't unduly concerned at that point because the idea was to run it for a bit of crack with Clarky. I had seen Bikila around the village but we didn't know one another and that was as near as we got to each other.

The race started with three laps of the track and then we headed out of the stadium on to the road. Oddly enough, Clarky and myself were in front. The pace was modest enough, especially for track runners, and we were moving along comfortably. At six miles, Bikila joined us so then there were three.

We were getting away from the rest of the field. At ten miles, Clarky began to drop back. When we reached the halfway mark (13.1 miles) Bikila was twenty metres in front. He was running very easily, a sight to behold. Not once did he look across at me; he was focused on the course in front and his head was rock-steady.

The atmosphere along the course was quite amazing, with over a million people lined up watching. They also had a train running by the side of the course, packed with people. We made the turn and I closed in on him but he just as easily began to move away again. At twenty miles his time was 1 hour 39 minutes. I went through in 1 hour 39 minutes 50 seconds. We both went under 1 hour 40 minutes, breaking the world record for twenty miles in the process – the famous Ethiopian, Bikila, tracked by an unknown in an Irish singlet.

At twenty-two miles, I was beginning to feel unwell. I had no drinks taken up to this point and I was beginning to struggle. At the twenty-three-mile mark, there was no way I could have carried on. I couldn't put one leg past the other and I had to pull out of the race.

As I'm sitting there on the side of the road who comes along but Clarky. He stands in the middle of the road doubled over in pain. He's finished too, I thought, he'll go no further. He managed to get himself going again and by Jesus he finished seventh, which was a fantastic performance for him. I could not understand how he was able to finish that race.

They got me back to the stadium, thanks to the help of the New Zealand people. There was no Irish official to be seen anywhere, at any time. Eventually I recovered and got back to the village and went to bed for a few hours. I recovered from the exhaustion fairly quickly but my legs were badly blistered.

I felt I ran a real good race, the way I wanted to run it. If the Irish doctor had paid more attention to me between the 10,000 metres and the marathon I believe I'd have finished second. I knew nothing about taking drinks before the race or the importance of hydration. No official bothered to ask about my welfare. The fact of the matter is that I never met an official or indeed any Irishman till I got back on the plane to go home.

People said afterwards that if I hadn't run so fast I would have finished. But I wouldn't. I reckon that in a marathon the speed you run at – unless you go mad altogether – doesn't make a lot of difference. It's the length of time you're on the road. It's easier to be out on the road for two hours running fast than for two-and-a-half hours running slowly. It's the extra time on the road that makes you tired. It could also be that I am viewing the marathon distance through the eyes of a track runner.

I learned some hard lessons during those Olympics. More important than anything else was knowing that I had a world-class marathon in me. If I could run that well in the condition I was in, I vowed that when I got a clear run for another marathon, I would definitely run a good one. I waited two years for that opportunity and the mistakes of Tokyo were not repeated. Hogan, I told myself, you'll never again quit in a race for want of a drink of water.

The Olympic Marathon...Irishman's Great Effort In Blistering Marathon...In Sight of A Medal – Then, He Faltered, Collapsed... Hogan's Gallant, Golden Bid Fails

It is now just on midnight and Tokyo is dying into quietness. I am a little quiet too, reflecting back on an extraordinary day which brought world records tumbling on all sides...which brought excitement that I will savour for many a day to come...and which brought a certain sporting tragedy as far as Ireland was concerned. We should now be proudly boasting two Olympic silver medals. But those two silver medals have disappeared into nothing and all we are left with now is the bronze medal Jim McCourt won [in boxing] on Tuesday night.

Had Jim Hogan's gamble succeeded in the marathon; had a little justice been done in the lightweight boxing semi-finals my story now would have been one of triumph. Instead, it must be one of a little sorrow.

I was a little bitter when Hogan dropped out of the 10,000 metres a week ago, but I must be honest and admit that no one tried harder and more courageously today in his bid to win us an Olympic medal in the marathon.

Hogan did not finish...but, just to put things straight, he did not fail. He gambled and lost...and, in losing, in this, his first ever marathon, he did almost as much as any Irish athlete has done in these games.

He ran himself to blistering exhaustion and then, with only a couple of miles to go, had to be carried off and taken on a stretcher to the Olympic Village hospital.

'I knew I had to redeem myself after the 10,000 metres,' he told me there, 'and I gave this race everything I had. I was within a few miles of a silver medal, or perhaps a bronze one, and I kept going until I collapsed.

'It came on me suddenly. I was a little tired but felt that I could keep going. Then I collapsed and that was that. I feel that I have redeemed myself.

'I was not interested in finishing far down the field just to earn a few sympathetic cheers when I arrived at the stadium. It had to be all or nothing and I am quite happy that I tried my best.'

And I can tell you that he did try his best until he collapsed. Up to then he had run the race of his life and in the process returned the second-fastest time ever recorded for twenty miles – a compelling indication of the punishing pace set by Ethiopian Abebe Bikila, the shock 1960 victor. A lesser man might have let Bikila get far away from him. Hogan might have slowed down his pace to a speed which would have ensured that he reached the finishing line. But as I said already, he gambled…and lost. Personally I think it was worth the gamble.

Jim suffered a lot of pain in defeat. He is still dreadfully tired and his feet are blistered and sore. One must not blame him for failing. Anyone who runs himself to exhaustion cannot be blamed too much.

Abebe Bikila is, of course, a remarkable man, particularly when one considers that in repeating his Rome success he set a world-best time and that he returned to training just eleven days after he had his appendix removed last month – little short of incredible!

Perhaps Hogan made a mistake in trying to match himself with Abebe. Had he, instead, matched himself with, say, Basil Heatley, who eventually finished second, the story might have been different. Hogan elected to try for the big prize and his great gamble failed. Had he finished second or third we would have been proud of him tonight. He failed to finish…but I still think we should be a little proud of him. He gave the best he had – but, that, unfortunately, was not enough.

Hogan set off at a brisk pace and was well up as the field when he disappeared into the tunnel and out of the stadium. Then we had to turn to the television sets on the edge of each press box to see the rest of this gruelling race – and what a 'grueller' it proved to be.

Over the first mile Hogan looked magnificent, with Australia's Ron Clarke and Britain's Ron Hill beside him. He pounded along steadily to the five-kilometre post which he reached in 15 minutes 8.0 seconds, a couple of seconds behind Clarke.

Shortly after that they were joined by the dark figure of the Ethiopian…and the pace was sustained even as the heat intensified. He led the field past the ten-kilometre post in 30 minutes 14 seconds. (Billy Mills, the USA's gold-medallist in the 10,000 metres final had a time of 28 minutes 24.4 seconds for this distance on the track.)

Bikila raced into a 100-yard lead nearing the half-way mark and here, when the Ethiopian stopped for a glass of water, Hogan tried to catch him…all to no avail. He was only six or seven yards away when Bikila stretched out in front again. Clarke followed them a minute further behind and obviously tiring. All our eyes were, however, glued to the tiny figure of Hogan on the screen as he went all out for a silver medal – the Ethiopian was a 'certainty' for the gold.

The camera trained on Abebe for two or three minutes. Running easily and with almost superhuman power, he drove along at a fantastic pace. He was relaxed and running so effortlessly.

Suddenly the cameras switched to Hogan. He was slowing down. He halted, walked a few yards, trotted another few yards, then tried to return to his original pace. But he failed.

The Japanese translator beside me gave the commentator's

message: 'Hogan has collapsed. He is out of the race.'

Anguished.

That was the last I saw of Hogan until I met him later in the day in hospital.

A few minutes later Abebe raced into the stadium below us and sprinted around the track to finish in the fastest time ever for the marathon…an incredible 2 hours 12 minutes 11.2 seconds. Just to show how fresh he was he trotted into the infield and proceeded to do a few exercises!

Kakichi Tsuburaya (Japan) was second into the stadium but right behind him came Basil Heatley (Britain). To a deafening ovation the little Japanese raced down the back stretch. But the cheers turned to warning cries and one felt the dismay and anguish that swept through this vast crowd as Heatley caught Tsuburaya at the second-last bend and raced away to take second place.

For half an hour afterwards there was a procession of runners into the stadium, twenty-third in the 'roll' being Blackrock County Louth-born Peter McArdle, running for the USA in 2 hours 26 minutes 24.4 seconds.

David Guiney, the Irish Press, *Thursday 22 October 1964*

6

A Record-Breaking Year, 1965

It was a bloody disgrace that our top marathon runner had to declare for England to achieve success. And he got fiercely criticised for it. History will show that between Ron Delany's gold in 1956 and Eamonn Coghlan's gold in 1983, Jim Hogan from Limerick was the only Irishman to win an athletics gold medal in a major championship. Matter a damn what singlet he wore. It was a triumph for Hogan and for Ireland, but few were willing to acknowledge it.' David Guiney

Before I won the 1966 gold medal, Maeve Kyle said, 'I don't care who wins the race, as long as it's not Jim Hogan.' She didn't like me either, by the sound of things, and I don't know why. What I do know, however, is that she won nothing at all when it came to the big championships.

I waited two years for my opportunity in the marathon distance and I was really ready when I went to the European Championships. But by that stage I was running for Britain. I'd had enough of the meanness of the Irish officials. I realised they were never going to do anything for me. My argument was solely with the officials; I got on great with all the Irish fellows, lovely lads all them. I couldn't say enough good things about them.

MAY 1965

JUNE. 1965

May 23. 8. 10m Steady. 5. 12m good. 22.

May 24. 8. 8m Easy. 4. 2mJog. 20×370 2mJog. 20.

May 25. 10 mile Easy. 10

May 26. 10 mile Easy. 10

May 27. 2mJog. 20×330 2mJog. 8mile 20

May 28. 8. 8m Jog. 4mJog. 2mFast. 2mJog. 16.

May 29. 12 mile on the Hills 12

May 30. 10 mile good 10

May 31. 12. 3mFast. 5. 4mJog. 12×550, 2mJog. 16.

June 1st 2mJog 2 Laps of Park. 4mJog 20.

Jun 2. 3mT. 5. 11 mile Steady 14

Jun 3. 12. 3mJog. 5. 6mJog. 3m. 18. 35 2m 14.

Jun 4. 12. 3mJog. 4. 9 mile Easy. 12

Jun 5. 9.45. 15 mile. Park. 6. 3mJog 18

Jun 6. 9. Jog 2m. 6×440. 1m Jog. 6

Jun 7. 6m Jog. 5m Fast. 1mJog. 12

Jun 8. 12. 5m good. 5. 20 mile. Park. 26

June 9. 12. 5m good. 5. 16 mile. Park 24

Jun 10. 12 4mJog 5. 2mJog. 8×440. 2mJog. 12

June 11. 12 3mJog. 4. 30. 13 mile say Park. 16.

June 12. 10. 30 11mg ood. 7m Fast Slow. 18.

June 13. 18 miles. Park Total 126 18

14. 12. 3mJog. 6. Jog. 4m. 12×500. 3mJog. 16.

15. 12 mile Steady 12

16. 12. 3mJog. 5. 30. 3mJog. 8×510. 3mJog 14.

17. 12 3mJog. 5. 3mJog. 6 mile good. 1mJog. 13.

18 12 3mJog. 2. 30 3m Jog 8×150 2mJog 12

19 7.15. 3mJog. 2. 6mJog. 3mFast. 1mJog 15

20. 9.30. 16 miles. Park. 5. 5 mile Easy. 21

21. 12. 3mJog. 5. 5mJog. 6mile 28 4. 1mJog 19

22. 22 miles Easy - Park. 22

23. 12. 3mJog. 5. 4m Jog. 10×440. 1m 12

24. 12 3m good. 5. 9 mile Steady 14

25 12. 2mJog 6×150. 1mJog 9. 3mJog 7

26. 8. 3mJog. 3. 6mJog. 2m Fast. 1mJog 12

27. 9. 30. 16m Park. 6. 4m Steady. 2

28. 12 1m. 3Fast. 1. 5. 3mJog. 6 Fast. 2mJog. 16

29. 22 miles - Park. 22

30. 12. 1Jog. 3 Fast. 1m. 5. 3mJog. 10×550 2mJog 1

1. 12. 3mJog. 5. 3mJog. 7mgood. 1mJog. 14

2. 12. 3mJog. 2. 30 2mJog 6×150 1mJog 8. 4mJog 12

3. 4 m Jog 2m Fast 2mJog 8

4. 18 miles - Park 6. 4 mile slow. 22

JULY 1965

July 26. AM 6. 1 Hour Jog. 8. 2M Jog a Beach. 10

July 27. 3pm 3 M Jog. PM 10. 4 M Jog. 3 M Fast. 1 M Jog 11 ITALY RACE

July 28.   Rest and Traveling

July 29. PM 12. 5 M Jog. PM 5. 4 M Jog. S/10 Jog 10X5/10 2 M Jog. 18

July 30. 12. PM 5 M Jog. 7. PM 6 M Easy.   11

July 31 AM 9. 11 miles i lehiand Here. Rent to City a Beach. 18

AUG 1st 18 miles in PARK   18 Total 86

AUG 2 12. PM 1 M Jog. 3 M good. 1 M Jog. 5. PM 7 M Jog   12.

AUG 3. 12. PM 4 M Steady. 8. 18 mile PARK   22.

AUG 4 12. PM 3 M Jog 5. PM 3 M Jog. 4/10 Jog 8X440 3 M Jog.   13.

AUG 5 PM 12. 3 M Jog 5. PM 3 M Jog 6 M good. 3 M Jog   15.

AUG 6. 12 PM 3 M Jog. 4. PM 1 M Jog 6X150 Jog 180 Jog 1 M Jog   6.

AUG 7.   2. 30. 4 M Jog 3 M Fast 1 M Jog 13 19.6   8 RACE MY BEST 3 mile
                                                                Total 92

AUG 8.   16 mile Steady.   16

AUG 9. 12 PM 4 M Jog. 5. PM 3 M Jog 6 M good. 2 M Jog   15

AUG 10. 12. 1 M Jog 3 M good. 1 M Jog 5 1/440 Jog 16 mile Steady. 21

AUG 11. 12. PM 4 M Jog. 5. PM 5 M Jog. 10X440 2 M Jog.   16

AUG 12. 12. 3 M Jog 5. 3 M good. 7 mile good. 2 M Jog   15

AUG 13.   4 mile Jog.   4.

AUG 14. AM 7. 2 M Jog. 1 4 M Jog. 6 M FAST. MINS 28 SEC 50 12 BRITISH 10000 M
                                                                RACE
                                                                RECORD

AUG 15   Jog. 1 Hour   10 Total 93

63

There was Tommo (Tom O'Riordan); he was class was Tommo, a lovely man from Kerry who went to the States on an athletic scholarship. You'd never know it though; he was a very modest bloke, a brilliant athlete, great crack after races, fond of a pint. I met his son Ian and he's a credit to his father and doing very well indeed. Bertie Messitt was another athlete I had tremendous respect for. There was several others. I think the athletes understood why I ran for Britain.

It all came to a head in Ostend, Belgium, in 1965. I'm flying over on the Saturday morning to run for Ireland – we had a good team, mind – and do you know what they wanted me to do: get in a boat on Thursday and go to Belgium and stay there for two days and miss two days' work when I could fly over in fifty minutes. I said, 'No, if you want me to run in Belgium you'll pay for my flight over.' And they wouldn't.

So I fly over to Belgium with my wife Mary and we're sitting above in the stands. I never ran. And of course they knew I was there. Somebody told them and they're walking up and down at the bottom of the stand looking for me and I above looking down on them. That's when I changed. I said to myself, 'What the hell am I doing here?'

Coming back from Tokyo the year before I had borrowed some money from another Irish athlete to take a direct flight from Frankfurt to London in order to get home faster to be with Mary. I rang up the ticket office to get a refund for the unused half of my London–Dublin return ticket and found that it had already been cashed in. The following March, a few days after Belgium, I finally received a cheque for the unused Dublin–London fare.

I decided then that this was the end of the road for Ireland as I never got any international races or recognition. I was never sent to any international event, even in Europe – they always seemed to pick fellows who were living in Ireland. It was as if I was an alien because I worked and ran in London. By this time I'd been living in London for so many years that I had no problem changing nationality. I got a British passport in order to run for Britain. I've never had an Irish passport since then, although I had one before that. I'd have loved to win the European Championship for Ireland if I had been allowed to do it.

I had a fantastic year in 1965. Every race I ran in was better than the last. There was a three-mile in Portsmouth where I finished second in 13 minutes 19.06 seconds, my best time over that distance, and of course the 10,000-metres British record at the White City on 14 August with a time of 28 minutes and 50 seconds. I also had several good races in Melbourne, Oslo and Siena, and I finished out that year by coming second in a 10,000-metres inter-city race between Milan and London, in 29 minutes 18.4 seconds. Consistency was the key for me that year.

I qualified to represent Britain in the marathon by coming second in the Poly Marathon – Windsor to Chiswick – on a very hot day, 11 June 1965, in a time of 2 hours, 19 minutes and 27 seconds. The sole of my foot was badly blistered when the insole of my new Tiger running shoes came undone because of the heat.

DATE	MEETINGS	EVENTS	TIME @ PLACING
JAN 22	RICHMOND	9 miles cross country.	1st 43.22.
JAN 28	AUCLAND. NEW ZEALAND	3. mile on GRASS.	1st 14.23
FEB. 1st	AUCLAND. NEW ZEALAND	5.000 METRES.	4th 14.21 IRISH RECORD
FEB. 10.	MELBOURNE. AUSTRALIA	1. Hour Run.	1st 12 mile 265 ye 2.NO FINISH 1 mile old Record
MAR. 13.	ILFORD	ROAD RELAY. 3¾ mile	2. 17.9
MAR. 27	COSFORD.	2 miles INDOOR.	5th 8.50 8 PB
APRIL 3rd	WEMBLEY.	2,000 yRDS. INDOOR.	6th 5.0.0 PB STAGE RECORD.
APRIL 10	LONDON TO BRIGHTON	4½ mile ROAD LEGS.	1st 20.41. TRACK RECORD
APRIL 24	PORTSMOUTH	6 miles Southern CHP	1st 28.27. TRACK & MEETING RECORD
MAY 5th	LEYTON.	3 miles. INVITATION	1. 13.31 MEETING RECORD
MAY. 8.	RICHMOND	1. MILE CRASS	1st 1.4.20.4
MAY 8th	RICHMOND	2. MILES TRACK	1st 9.8.6 TRACK RECORD
JUNE 19	MOTSPUR PARK	3 miles Southern CHP.	1st 13.27.6. 3/4 FORCE WIND.
JUNE 26.	SOUTH SHIELDS	2 MILES INVITATION	2NO 9.4.
JULY 3rd	BRISTOL	2 MILES. INVITATION	2NO 8.43.0 PB
JULY 9th	WHITE CITY	6 MILES. A.A.A.	4th 27.44.8
JULY 14.	OSLO	10.000 METERES	2NO 29.19.6 PB
JULY 16.	PARIS	5,000 METRES.	5. 13.57.9 PS
JULY 25	SEINA. ITALY.	10,000 METRES	1st 29.34 MEETING Record, 90%
JULY 27	CROSSATA. ITALY.	5.000 METRES.	3rd 14.5.2.
JUNE	WHITE CITY	6 mile INTER Co DID NOT FINISH	

Jim's racing record for the first half of 1965.

JIM HOGAN

answers the A.W. Questionnaire

Jim Hogan wins the Southern 3 miles by 30 yards in 13:27.6—his most pleasing performance.

Ed Lacey

Full name:
James Joseph Hogan.

Birthplace & date:
Croom, Co.Limerick (RoI), 28.5.33.

Height & weight:
5'9½", 132lb.

Club:
Polytechnic Harriers.

Occupation:
Groundsman.

Personal best marks:
Mile—4:08.3 time-trial (1963), 2M—8:43.0 (1965), 3M—13:19.6 (1965), 5000m—13:57.4 (1965), 6M—27:35.0 (1964), 10,000m—28:50.0 (1965), 1 hour—12M 275y (1965).

Which performance has given you most pleasure?
Southern 3 miles win this year. Because it was my first race after my having to drop out in the inter-counties 6 miles, and also because I beat a very good field of three-milers who were scared to have a go until I ran away from them with six laps to go.

How many days a week do you train?
Seven all year round.

At what time of day do you normally train?
12 noon and 5 p.m.

How long are your training sessions?
40 minutes at noon, 1-1½ hours in evening.

Please describe your warmup:
For training: I run easily for about 20 min., a few exercises and then I am ready, For competition: I warm up for about one hour. I jog very easily for about 20 min., then I do some exercises, a few easy strides and change into my racing gear (I never warm up in what I race in). I then jog until the start of my event.

Please give details of a typical week's training in winter:
Monday: (Noon) 4-5 miles on road, whatever speed I feel like. (5 p.m.) 15 miles on road at a good speed if I feel good.
Tuesday: (Noon) 10-12 miles on road, fast and slow after Christmas, steady before Christmas.
Wednesday: (Noon) 4-5 miles in the woods where I work. (5 p.m.) 3 miles warmup; 12 or 15x440 on grass; 3 miles jogging.
Thursday: (Noon) mile warmup; 3 miles fast; 1 mile warm-down. (5 p.m.) 1 hour easy if I am

Sunday: (9.30 a.m.) 15-20 miles with other athletes.

Please give details of any weight training:
So far I have done no weight training, but I may do some this winter. It may help my finish.

Name of coach:
I have no coach, but Gordon Pirie has helped me.

How much of your success is due to coaching?
Coaching has not helped me very much. To me, a coach is someone an athlete makes and then he uses this top athlete to boost his name. At 27 years of age my best 6 miles time was 30:12 and I have improved to my present standard by dedication, hard work and the will to keep going despite bad injuries and other setbacks.

How many days rest do you like before competition?
I never rest before competition, but may ease my training a little.

How often do you like to compete?
In summer I do not like to compete very often, once a week is enough—but this year I did run four 6 miles races and three 3 miles races in a 27-day period. This is not easy to do and I would not advise it unless you are a Ron or Parke.

racing on Saturday; otherwise same as Monday.
Friday: (Noon) 30 min. easy running if racing on Saturday; otherwise same as Wednesday. (4.30 p.m.) A few easy strides if racing on Saturday; otherwise same as Wednesday.
Saturday: If racing, I run for 30 min. in morning; if not, I do a 15 miles run in the park.
Sunday: 18-22 miles steady run on the road and in the park.

Please give details of a typical week's training in summer:
Monday: (Noon) 4-5 miles easy in woods. (5 p.m.) 4 miles warmup; 12x500 on grass, quite fast with 500 jog in between; 3 miles warm-down.
Tuesday: (Noon) Same as Monday. (5 p.m.) Sometimes have a 6 miles time-trial; otherwise 15-18 miles in Richmond Park.
Wednesday: (Noon) Same as Monday. (5 p.m.) 1½ hours steady running on grass.
Thursday: (Noon) Same as Monday. (5 p.m.) 3 miles warmup; 6 miles quite fast in woods; 2 miles warm-down.
Friday: (Noon) If racing on Saturday—2 miles warmup, 4 or 6x440 at 65-66 speed, 2 miles warm-down; no running in evening. If not racing, I sometimes do 30x440 (66-67), with 110 jog recovery.
Saturday: If racing, I run easily for 30 min. in morning. If not racing, I run 15-22 miles in Richmond Park.

What are your goals in athletics?
Next year I want to make the English and British teams for the Commonwealth Games and European Championships, and run 13:10 for 3 miles and 27:20 for 6 miles. Ultimately, to break a long distance world record and run a marathon inside 2:10 if I can find the time to train for one.

What advice would you offer the young athlete or novice?
First he must remember there is no short cut to the top and that it may take a long time to achieve this. He must work hard over a long period and take the rough with the smooth. Never get a big head because you are as good as your last race, and if you have a bad one this is what everyone remembers—not the good runs you had but the one bad run. So I say once again to young athletes, work hard and have faith in yourself at all times.

Any further comments?
I would like to see more indoor tracks where athletes could train on cold winter evenings as cold weather helps bring on injuries and other setbacks. When I retire from running I would like to help 3 and 6 miles runners if they were prepared to work hard and seek my advice.

Athletics Weekly questionnaire, 1965.

Vol. 19   No. 34
August 21st, 1965   THE ATHLETE'S MAGAZINE

Jim Hogan is second to Fergus Murray in the three-mile at Portsmouth on 7 August 1965. His time of 13 minutes 19.6 seconds was his fastest ever at this distance.

*Running barefoot, Jim Hogan breaks the British 10,000-metres record
at the White City on 14 August 1965 in a time of 28 minutes 50 seconds.*

7

Marathon Gold:
The European Championships, Budapest, 1966

Hogan a Must for Athletics in Lille

Will the AAU selectors remember Jim Hogan when they meet this week to name the four-man Irish team for the 13th International La Voix du Nord race in Lille, France, on 17 January?

Hogan, the fastest Irishman ever over six miles, came in for criticism when his Olympic 'gamble' failed.

Hogan, in fairness, himself criticised the AAU before he left for Tokyo, pointing out that they had not included him in the teams for this summer's international matches although he was a world-ranked six-miler.

Hogan finished fifth in the International Cross-Country Championship race in Leopardstown in March, and when I contacted him in London this week he said he was back in training and fully recovered from his Olympic ordeal.

He deserves his place in the Irish team for Lille, if only to get the opportunity to redeem himself.

Evening Press, *December 1965*

The Irish newspapers may have been writing what suited them, but they surely didn't know anything about my intentions. I had already made up my mind that I would not run for Ireland again while it was governed by those miserable bastards. It was typical of them to say nothing to the press, leaving the public to believe that I was the guilty party in the whole mess. It was a bit late in the game to be writing about redemption anyway. I never felt that I had to redeem myself over my performances in Tokyo. I stopped reading the Irish papers; in fact I stopped reading anything about athletics in order to focus on my main goal for 1966 – the marathon.

FINAL WEEK OF TRAINING BEFORE BUDAPEST

1 August	18 miles in Richmond Park.
2 August	(lunchtime) 3 miles easy running.
(4.30pm)	15 Miles in Richmond Park.
3 August	(lunchtime) 4 miles easy.
(4.30pm)	15 miles fast on hilly course in 75 minutes.
4 August	(lunchtime) 3 miles easy.
(4.30pm)	3 mile warm-up, 6 miles fast, 3 miles warm-down, all on grass.
5 August	Lunchtime 5 miles easy.
(4.30pm)	3.5 miles easy. 8x500 yards fast with 400-yard jog. 2.5 miles warm-down.
6 August	(8.00pm) 1 mile warm-up, 7 miles fast, 1 mile warm-down.
7 August	(7.00am) 7 miles easy.
Total for week	99 miles.

1966

DATE	MEETINGS	EVENS	TIME and PLACING
JAN. 8.	RICHMOND.	5. miles Cross-Country	1st 23. 45. Record.
JAN 22	RICHMOND	9. Miles Cross Country	1st 43. 25.
JAN 30.	SAN SEBASTIAN	10000 metre Cross.	6th 31. 33. 1st EUROPEAN @ U.K Record
FEB 5.	COSFORT.	3 mile Indoor.	1. 13. 37. Record.
FEB 26.	CHISWICK	5½ ROAD RACE.	1st 25. 56
MARCH. 5	SHEFFIELD	9 miles NATIONAL CROSS.	3rd 46. 48.
MARCH. 12.	ILFORD.	3¾ miles Road Relay	1st 17. 4.
MARCH 26.	BRUSSELLS.	10500. Cross-Country metres	21st
APRIL 23	MOTSPUR PARK	6. Miles Southern C.P.	1st 28. 31. 8 TRACK RECORD
APRIL 30	OXFORD.	3 mile	2nd 13. 45 Bad Run.
MAY. 2st	PADDINGTON	6 miles MIDDLESEX	1st 29. 2. 6
MAY 7th	RICHMOND	2 miles P. M 2. 40	1st 9. 7. 0
MAY 7.	RICHMOND	1. mile P. M 4. 10.	1st 4. 24. 0
MAY. 14.	SOUTHALL.	2. MILES	1st 8. 57. TRACK RECORD
MAY 18	CHISWICK	1 mile club CHP.	1st 4. 18. 3
MAY 21st	FELTHAM.	3 mile MIDDUX CHP.	2nd 13. 41. 6 BAD Run
MAY. 30.	WHITE CITY.	6 miles BRITISH GAMES	4th 28. 10. 4 P. B
JUNE 11.	WINDSOR To CHISWICK	26. 385 MAR. mile YRDS	2nd 2. 19. 27 P.B
JUNE 22.	CRYSTAL PALACE.	5,000 metres.	10. 13. 57.
JUNE 24.	WELWYN.	2. miles	2nd 8. 57

Above and facing, Jim Hogan's race results for 1966, the year he won marathon gold in the European Championships in Budapest,

DATE	MEETING	EVENT	TIME and PLACING
JUNE 26	LUTON.	3. MILES	2.ⁿᵈ 13. 41. 8 windy.
JULY 8ᵗʰ	WHITE CITY	6 MILES	11.ᵗʰ 27. 53. 4 18.16 B.B of 4 mile
July 31ˢᵗ	MIKKELIN	3,000. METRES	7.ᵗʰ 8. 16. 4 TRACK RECORD.
AUG 3ʳᵈ	KOUVOLA	10,000 METRES	1ˢᵗ 29. 18. 4
AUG 7ᵗʰ	TURKU.	5,000 METRES	1ˢᵗ 14. 0. 2
AUG 20ᵗʰ	WHITE CITY	5,000 METRES.	7.ᵗʰ 14. 7. 0 Hours Mins Sec
SEPT.4ᵗʰ	BUDAPEST	EUROPEAN MARATHON	1ˢᵗ 2. 20. 4 GOLD
SEPT. 10ᵗʰ	CARDIFF	3 MILES WELSH GAMES	2.ⁿᵈ 13. 45. 6
SEPT. 15ᵗʰ	OSTRAVA.	3,000 METRES ARMY CHPS	3.ʳᵈ 8. 24. 6
SEPT 16ᵗʰ	BANO.	5,000 METRES	1ˢᵗ 14. 17. 6.
SEPT 19ᵗʰ	PRAGUE	RUDUE DE PRAVO ROADRACE	9.ᵗʰ 17. 14. 2 stage RECOR
SEPT. 25	HORNCHURCH	6 mile, ROAD RELAY.	1ˢᵗ 27. 40. NEW RECORD
Oct. 8ᵗʰ	BELGRAVE.	5 mile, ROAD RELAY	1ˢᵗ 24. 12. RECORD
OCT 22.	BRISTA	5¼ MILES RoadRelay	1ˢᵗ 24. 39. NEW WORLD RECOR
NOV 12.	WALTON.	30,000. METRES.	1. 1 32. 25. 4
NOV 27ᵗʰ	JAPAN.	MARATHON.	FELL when lying 3ʳᵈ at 20 km VERY WET.
DEC. 10ᵗʰ	RICHMOND.	7 miles Cross Country.	1ˢᵗ 34. 18
		1ˢᵗ 20.	2.ⁿᵈ 6. 3.ʳᵈ 2. 4.ᵗʰ 1
	UNPLACED. 6.	MY BEST YEAR YET.	BRITISH BEST FOR 4 mile 18.16 Min Sec
WON THE	EUROPEAN MARATHON CHAMPIONSHIP		IN BUDAPEST. SEPT 3rd
BROKE	THE WORLD RECORD FOR 3,0000 METRES AT WALTON Nov 12ᵗʰ Hour Mini Secs TIME 1. 32 25.4		
	EUROPEAN RECORD 3 mile INDOOR 13.3Y		

I thought Budapest was a beautiful city. I loved everything about it and my preparations went smoothly. In truth, I never liked running marathons – the 10,000 metres would have been my preferred event – but I wasn't going to get much faster over the shorter distance. British 10,000-metres runners even in those days weren't fast enough over the last couple of laps, when all the racing is being done.

On the Tuesday night before I left for Budapest I ran a fifteen-mile course that includes three big hills. Gerry North, a fine athlete, had run it with me two weeks before in 78 minutes and he said to me, 'Jesus, Jim, you're flying.' This time I went round in 75, and my self-confidence was sky-high. If anybody is going to beat me now, I thought, by Jesus they'll have to be motoring it. I had also been running fast on the track in the lead-up, with some really good 5000 metres and 10,000-metres races.

On the Sunday in Budapest (28 August) I trained with some of the boys, including Jim Alder and Dick Taylor, and they remarked on how well I was running. We stayed in the camp about fifteen miles outside Budapest. On the Monday I trained with Derek Graham. We ran five miles fast and he said he had never run so fast in training, and yet I wasn't really going all-out. I also trained with Alan Simpson, the British miler, and he said to me, 'You're the fittest man on this team, there's nobody fitter. When you get to eighteen miles you'll just wave them goodbye.' I didn't plan it that way, but that's how it went. [Alan Simpson had finished fourth in the 1500-metres Olympic Final in Tokyo 1964. Peter Snell (NZ) won gold in 3 minutes 38 seconds. John Davies, also of NZ, took the bronze medal in 3 minutes 39.6 seconds. Simpson finished agonisingly close in fourth position, a mere one-tenth of a second behind, in 3 minutes 39.7 seconds.]

From then on I just took it easy. I didn't train on Friday but trained for forty minutes on the Saturday, the day before the race, which was on 4 September. I was further encouraged by hearing that Mary was in good health back in England.

I had been eating a lot all week trying to get as strong as I could. I was also very well hydrated. I warmed up for about twenty-five minutes before the marathon and got a stitch! I didn't panic, though, and after doing some exercises and stretches I got rid of it. Once the race started I had no worries at all. At the turn my breathing was easy, while the other five or six around at that stage were all running hard and some were labouring.

At thirty kilometres (eighteen miles) there were five of us jostling for position as we approached a drinks table. I grabbed one and it fell out of my hand or something and I just carried on running. I got about twenty-five yards on them and didn't increase my pace at all. I expected to see them coming up on my shoulder but I was away.

After about three quarters-quarters of a mile I realised they weren't closing in. This is it now, I thought, and put the boot down. I ran the next five thousand metres faster than any of the previous, and the gap lengthened. The race was effectively over at this point, but I kept the pressure on.

At thirty-five kilometres (twenty-two miles) I went for a drink, although I didn't want to slow down because when you're tiring you don't like to break stride. I grabbed the drink and it slipped again! But it didn't matter for I grabbed a sponge, which is just as good as a drink, about sixty yards down the road.

The worst part was between twenty-three and twenty-five miles. There were two miles of dead straight road; you couldn't see the end. But I was going at a good pace and although I wouldn't look back I realised I had the race. I remember looking at the flags in the stadium in the distance. Next thing I know, a friend of mine, Charlie Dibbs from Belgrave Harriers, jumps out in the middle of the road 300 yards from the stadium entrance and shouts, 'You're home, there's nobody in sight.' I was over 600 yards ahead, 1 minute and 43 seconds.

I entered the stadium alone and got a terrific reception. I learned later that Billy Morton was in the press box, jumping up and own telling everyone, 'He's Irish you know, he's Irish.' That was typical of Billy, who always treated me very well.

Nobody's ever heard the story from my side. They've just heard what a bastard Jim Hogan was going off and running for the Brits. But Gaston Roelants, the Belgian running legend said to me: 'Look, Jim, if you never again win a race you've won the gold today. They can't take it off you.'

Mary sat at home during all this. There was a little bit of it on television. Norman Barnes, then writing for *The Times*, lived not too far from my home. He ran round to tell Mary the result of the race, in case she hadn't got it. It was a great moment for her, a proud moment. She knew what it meant to me. It wasn't an Olympic gold medal but it was my Olympics

European marathon gold for Jim Hogan, Budapest, 4 September 1966,
in a time of 2 hours, 20 minutes 4 seconds.

and a gold medal. I thought on the night and many times afterwards that few athletes could have beaten me.

If I'd had that fitness and preparation for the Olympics, I'm certain I would have had a silver medal. Bikila, in fairness, was unbeatable, but I'll tell you one thing: he wouldn't have dropped me so easily had I been better prepared. I would have stayed on his shoulder deeper into the race and made him earn it.

I wasn't pushed at all in Budapest and there was plenty left in the tank. If I had been challenged, I could certainly have taken it three minutes lower. I was full of energy after the race and on an impulse decided that I would copy Bikila and do some calisthenics. I wasn't trying to show off or anything like that. The crowd responded well to it anyway.

I've no regrets about the way things turned out for me. That's sport and there are no guarantees. You take what you're given.

At the medal ceremony I stood for the British national anthem, as the Union Jack was raised. It was a proud moment for me, a moment I'll treasure forever. And why wouldn't I? I'd no problem doing it. I stood there as a British subject. That country was kind to me and my wife and gave me a good way of life. I got nothing at all in Ireland by way of work and definitely not in athletics. I felt you should support the country you live and work in. I went to England with thousands upon thousands of others and I was thankful for it. I don't know how it went down in Ireland and I didn't rightly care. I do know that my own people in County Limerick didn't forget me. They had bonfires all over the place; the hills of Dromin and Athlacca were ablaze.

'Congratulations. You made Ireland proud,' Billy Morton wrote in a telegram. I got several wires congratulating me from people in Ireland. I know there was resentment and anger and a lot of ugly talk going around as well. But no one ever had the guts or honesty to say anything to my face. They would have got my respect if they had.

I was back in Tralee at the races in recent years and wearing my British blazer. This was before the peace settlement. An acquaintance took offence because I was wearing a British symbol and said, 'You shouldn't be wearing that around here – in north Kerry of all places. You could get in a lot of trouble around here for doing that.' I told him where to go, and what to do with himself too. I earned that blazer and I was going to wear it anywhere I pleased. I never went looking for trouble but I tell you I was never frightened of any man, either in athletics or in life.

'As far as I'm concerned, passion defines the best of us.'
(Steve Scott, American miler, personal best 3 minutes 7.69 seconds, Oslo Olympics, 7 July 1982, twice US Olympian 1,500 metres and cancer survivor)

When you get to that stage of your athletic career you run for yourself. Any athlete will tell you that if they're honest. You're not running for your country or your club, you're running for you, because if you're injured tomorrow you don't get any of these fellows coming and telling you how great you are and offering to pay for your physiotherapy.

What is the essential running talent really? It might be the gift of speed in the muscles, a good set of lungs or a lot of other little things. Talent on its own never won a race. It comes down to hard work, repetitive hard work. And you have to want to win it badly enough. You have to be a bit of a madman because there are risks every time you step on the track.

Forget about your clubs and your countries and your loyalties. Above all else you must have a love of running, and I had that. As hard as the athletic life was at that time, I wouldn't have traded it for comfort or security.

I lived for that challenge, testing myself after taking the starting line. For me there was nothing that came remotely close to that. People might look differently at wins, records, medals and the even the athlete himself, if they had any clue about the motivation that drives it all. I still run or jog to this day. Not every day, mind you, but I do like to get out there alone in the woods or in some nice grassy field. At heart I still feel like the athlete, racing around the track, remembering the old days when racing was satisfying and fresh, the same each day but always a little different and exciting.

On 12 November 1966 I decided to go for the world record in the 30-kilometre track race in Walton-on-Thames. I won the race in 1 hour, 32 minutes and 25.4 seconds, beating the world record by nine seconds. I remember that the day was cold and wintry and the track wasn't great either but I had planned this attempt for a few years and had a feeling that I would be able to break the world record.

Jim Hogan on his world-record-breaking 30-kilometres run on 12 November 1966.

In general, 1967 was a quiet year. I did make the British cross-country team but I was disqualified for missing out on some artificial obstacles they had put in. I finished fifth. I was quite upset over the disqualification at the time and said so, as you can see in the following newspaper report:

Hogan Wants Medal

Limerick born Jim Hogan was yesterday still unrepentant, despite having been the first man ever to be disqualified in the sixty-four-year-old history of the international cross-country championships.

The 'H' (for Hogan) bomb of the athletics world exploded last Saturday when Jim was ruled out for failing to cross some of the hurdles dotted on the 7.5-mile course at Barry, Glamorgan.

Hogan was second man home in England's winning team until he was disqualified for evading obstacles. He reckons he is entitled to one of the medals handed out to the first six.

Declares the controversial Mr H.: 'If the sixth man is a sport, he will give me his medal.'

Course umpires decided not that Hogan missed hurdles but that he pushed officials out of his path and so imperiled England's chances of taking the team title for the fourth year running.

The course, containing hurdles and a water jump, was really a steeplechaser's paradise and not a cross-country race.

Belgium's Olympic champion Gaston Roelants proved that when romping home first in 36 minutes 2 seconds after a powerful display of front-running.

Hogan is European marathon champion and even before the headline-hitting Barry event, he was concerned about the obstacles.

That was a controversy that I would have preferred to avoid but things settled after that and I began to think ahead to the 1968 Olympics in Mexico City.

8

THE MEXICO OLYMPICS, 1968

After winning the gold medal in the European Championships I might have been expected to suffer a bit of a let-down. I'm not certain that was the case; I certainly didn't feel that way and I had high hopes facing into the two years before Mexico. Being European Champion didn't change me in any noticeable way but I did feel that on any given day under the right conditions, I could run with the best of them.

It was a conviction I never shared with anyone because athletics can pull the rug out from under you when you least expect it. Knowing that kept me fairly level-headed and the competition for places in any British team was red hot. There was a huge depth of talent in the middle distances, so you could never take any race or opponent for granted. I trained on in 1967 and it was quite a good year for me. There was that controversy over the cross-country disqualification but I wasn't going to hammer myself in cross-country anyway.

We prepared for Mexico and I qualified for the 10,000 metres, running the fastest time in my life, going through six miles in 27 minutes 30 seconds. There were really only five in contention, and three of us were marathon runners so we were able to divide up the race between us.

I ran the trial for the marathon but dropped out. Ron Hill and I took the field through ten miles in forty-nine minutes, roughly 4 minutes 54 seconds mile pace. That was madness, but we didn't slow at all. Up hill and down dale the two of us went at it, maintaining this unbelievable speed. Two madmen! Something had to give and I tossed away any chance because of that pace.

Tim Johnson won it; Bill Alcocks got second, and Ronnie (Hill) took third and the final place on the marathon team. (In 1970, Ron Hill won the Boston Marathon, and shattered the course record by three minutes, in a time of 2 minutes 10.3 seconds. In July of that year at the Commonwealth Games in Edinburgh, Hill took the gold medal in the marathon, becoming the second man and first Briton to break the 2-minutes-10-second barrier. His time was 2 minutes 9.28 seconds.)

Looking back I might have been better off in the marathon in Mexico because you had to go that bit slower at altitude, whereas the 10,000 metres was run faster and it was harder to run at that pace. Running at altitude was a new experience, not a very pleasant one to be honest. When we went to train in Mexico, it seemed to be easier to run on the roads. This was very noticeable when you were away from the track and everything else. You could actually get a fourteen or fifteen-mile run in, away from the confinement of the Olympic village. I felt that this confinement made the effects of the altitude a lot worse.

In the 10,000 metres final, the Africans ran away with the race: Naftali Temu of Kenya won gold in 29 minutes 27.4

seconds; Mamo Wolde of Ethiopia won silver in 29 minutes 28 seconds and Tunisia's Mohamed Gammoudi won bronze in 29 minutes 34.2 seconds. I didn't stand a chance and came in twenty-sixth in the field of thirty-plus runners.

THREE CHEERS FOR THE BULL!

We did get to do a lot of sightseeing and socialising in Mexico and I was always glad that I made the most of those opportunities. One of the highlights for me anyway was the day we went to a bullfight in Mexico City. You had massive crowds in a festive kind of mood, all roaring and shouting at the bull. That poor bull had no chance. He was dead before the bloke came in to stab him.

All of a sudden this fellow comes in and kneels down in the middle of the ring all decked out in his finery, a real cocky bloke altogether. He has this red flag in front of him and he's taunting the bull. Well, as sure as I'm standing here now, the bull made a drive for him and drove him thirty feet into the air.

When he hit the ground he was a dead as a doornail. So I jumped up and I shouted: 'Three Cheers For The Bull!' and the whole place went silent. There wasn't a murmur in the crowd.

I could tell they were wondering who this madman shouting about the bull was. I told them who the madman was, though – the fellow laid out on the ground killed stone dead. It's a sporting thing for the Mexicans, part of their culture and tradition, but I saw nothing but vicious cruelty in it and I never again want to witness an event like that.

9

AFTER MEXICO

I ran in 1969, just average running, and I won six races – not too bad considering that I was suffering from an injury. The last race I won was in Walton Athletic Club on 10 September, 5000 metres in 14 minutes 33 seconds, a slow time for me. I had said to myself that the first time I couldn't break fourteen minutes for three miles, I'd give it up (5000 metres is 240 yards further than three miles).

It was an easy decision for me to retire. Age was catching up with me and if I couldn't run to a decent competitive standard I didn't want to be out there. I still ran and kept myself fairly fit but my racing days were over, or so I thought.

With the advent of the veterans' championships there were fellows coming out of the woodwork to try their luck. In most cases these were blokes who weren't good enough to go near open competition in their prime. I've nothing against veterans' competitions if that's what a bloke wants to do with his time. More luck to him.

Before I made a comeback in 1983 I had massive doubts about whether or not it was worth the bother. There was one factor that influenced me more than anything else, and that was my training. When I got back a measure of race fitness the training I did at the age of fifty was unbelievable. It was high quality and I was blown away by what I was able to do. Because of that I decided to give the veterans' scene a go and see what I could do with it. If you had told me in 1970 that I would be in serious training at the age of fifty I would have said you were completely off your game.

There was also the attraction of going to South America, where the championships were to be held. There was a collection made by many of my friends in the horse industry to help defray expenses, so I felt I had to go and honour their commitment to me. It still took me a while to get my head around the whole thing.

I had a lovely place to train in England – about a mile and a half a circuit. I used to divide it up into 3x500 metres and 2x400 metres and I'd cover four laps. I'd wind up doing 12x500 metres and 8x400 metres; in total I was running more than six miles inside forty-one minutes doing this interval training.

I went to America first of all and stayed in New York for twelve days. I went down to White Plains and got to talk with some of the other veterans. They were primarily interested in what age-group I was in. The training was going well and we'd be doing bunches of 400-metre laps in seventy seconds, no problem at all. I think being away from competitive running for more than ten years gave me a renewed freshness. But this only lasted for twelve months; then the injuries started due to the age factor. You can't trick your body when you get beyond a certain age, no matter what kind of training you're doing.

WORLD VETERAN CHAMPIONSHIPS 1983

I was entered for the 5000 metres and the cross-country race in the 1983 championships in Puerto Rico. I won the 5000 metres and the way I looked at it, it would be a bonus if I won the cross-country race as well. The weather was not in any way favourable to performing well. Conditions were brutal with temperatures 90°F and above and 85% humidity. We ran four age groups together – over forty, over forty-five, over fifty, over fifty-five. I decided to run steady and sensibly (this wasn't the Olympics!) and come through, and if I had to I'd drop out. The course was over golf courses and that kind of terrain. As the race progressed, I just kept picking people off and ended up third overall. I was beaten by two forty-year-olds.

I won the British Veterans' 5000 metres in Wolverhampton and locked horns with a bloke called Maurice Morrell from Wirral AC who was second in the race. Two years later I ran in the championships in Rome, I was unlucky in the 10,000 metres because they mixed up the lap count, and they made me run an extra lap in the heats. I lapped everybody in the field and some of them twice but it didn't do me any good as veteran racing goes on time and I was already finished.

I had been waiting for two years for a chance to race Morrell. I sat on him all the time until 600 metres out, and then I blasted him out of it, destroyed him. I got immense satisfaction from that but I knew that was the end of my brief flirtation with the veterans' scene.

I have no regrets about competing in those championships but as I've said elsewhere, I have no great respect for that kind of competition, and even if the injuries didn't set in, it was next to impossible to get motivated and worked-up about them. I'd had my time when I was younger and able to compete against the very best. Nothing could ever get near to that kind of experience, not for me anyway.

I could never get my head around the veteran scene. I have no time for it really and I get a bit disgusted when I see fellows my age out there competing. I have nothing against running to stay in shape and for health reasons. But I did my running when I was at my peak and anything after that was a letdown, a bit artificial to be honest. When I'm asked about my running career I do not include the veteran wins since they meant nothing to me personally. My running career effectively ended when I no longer felt good enough to race in open competition.

10

'We're Going to Go Home to Ireland'

I had absolutely no intention of ever leaving England until one morning Mary said to me, 'We're going to go home to Ireland.' It was only then I realised what was happening. I rang Declan Murphy in Newmarket and asked him to meet me. He knew it was serious when I wouldn't discuss it over the phone. I met him on a Sunday and I told him we were going home to live in Ireland. He just sat there stunned. He couldn't believe it. 'Jesus, why are you doing that?' he said after a few moments. Then I explained to him about Mary's wishes.

Over time I began to see the thinking and wisdom behind Mary's decision to return home. I think she did it all with me in mind, a totally selfless act and so typical of her. In any case, it was the best decision she ever made, and as it worked out, it was the best possible move for me. She definitely had a sense that it was the right thing to do. My only regret is that she didn't live long enough to enjoy our new home in Knocklong.

She realised that she was seriously ill before any of us became aware of it. In the back of her mind she must have thought that I'd have a better chance in Ireland if she was gone. She always said she wouldn't reach seventy and she died at sixty-nine. She suffered a lot but never complained. She also had some terrible falls. The worst one happened when I was on my way back from Gowran Park races. The phone rang and I was told that she'd had a bad fall and had been taken to the Regional Hospital in Limerick.

The day of the race meeting, Enda Bolger rang me and asked me would I take in a horse for him that was having an operation up in the Curragh. I agreed to do it after I checked that the gates were open, especially the middle gates, so that the man who was bringing the horse would be able to get in. The front gate was open but sure enough the middle gate wasn't. I rang Mary and asked her if she would go out and open the middle gate; she was still walking around at the time.

She went out to open the gate and while doing so she noticed that the stable door was closed. It's a stiff door. She pulled the door towards her but it came quickly and unexpectedly, knocking her down. She fractured her hip and couldn't move. She remained on the ground helpless for nearly two hours until Joe Mitchell came with the horse. He lifted her up and got her into the house and then called Dr Cleary, a friend of his. After he arrived an ambulance was called and they took her to the hospital.

When I got to the hospital, they still hadn't done a thing for her. She was lying on one of those stretchers in the A&E. Eventually they got around to her. They had to operate on her hip. She got through that okay but the healing was very slow. As she said herself, it could have been a lot worse. Luckily the evening was dry. Had it been raining God only knows what would have happened. It was a freak accident but it left its mark on her. It's hard to say if she ever fully recovered from the shock of the fall. Breaking her hip certainly didn't help her overall condition.

MARY'S ILLNESS

When Mary was diagnosed with Parkinson's, it was like reading a death sentence. I was told that the disease 'causes a progressive loss of nerve cell function in the front of the brain that controls muscle movement. Progressive means that this disease's effects get worse over time. People who have PD experience tremors or shaking as a result of the damage to their nerve cells. The tremors may affect one side of the body more than the other, the lower jaw, arms and legs.'

'Nightmares, depression, difficulty walking or buttoning clothes…There is no cure for PD.' I cried at first when I knew what was in store for her and vowed to fight it every step of the way. As I learnt from watching her deteriorate, there was nothing at all I could do to ease the burden. I would have taken on her illness in a heartbeat. Hasn't she already suffered enough, I thought.

As always, Mary fought quietly and showed a super attitude when visitors came. 'How are you, Mary?' people would ask. 'I'm good. I'm very well, thank you. And how are you and your family getting on? Is your mother any better?' She would deflect attention away from herself every time.

When the illness began to take its toll on her body she never once complained. Before the end she couldn't eat, she couldn't speak. She was mad to smoke and she couldn't hold a cigarette. It was a terrible thing to watch and not be able to do anything except bathe her and try and comfort her in any possible way. The illness had taken everything: her walk, her talk and finally her life…It was devastating. I wouldn't wish it on my worst enemy.

Living Alone

Mary was a terrible loss to me but I made up my mind there and then that I'd have to keep going without her. There's no good sitting inside looking at four walls. Mary would not have wanted that at all at all and I wouldn't dishonour her memory by giving in to grief and loneliness. At the time of her death, I had some horses and I was riding out for a few people, so I just kept on doing that.

I won't tell you a word of a lie but it was hard, at times very hard, but I kept going. Mary knew that my brothers and sisters and their children were living not too far from Knocklong. And we had set up a lovely place to live with plenty of fields and room to relax. There was just no question of not getting on with it.

I believe she knew what was going to happen, and she got me sorted and in a situation where I was able to carry on after her death. I've no doubt about that.

This is from an interview with me to which Mary contributed. I'm not sure of the background to it, but she answered the question thoughtfully and with honesty, so typical of her. Hearing it for the first time recently was quite startling, a bit emotional. A lot of memories came flooding back. I was hesitant to use it in the book but it gives the reader a good idea of the marvellous character of the woman.

'You asked if I remember any resentment toward Hogan (I often refer to him in that way) when he ran for Britain. There may have been resentment among the Irish but I wouldn't know anything about that. I kept away from the Irish in England as best I could. I did not belong to any clubs or frequent any dance halls.

'I believe that if the English people were going to pay my living, I owed my loyalties to them and to no one else. I fully supported my husband in his athletic endeavours, and by and large I let him do his own thing. I was very proud of him when he won the gold medal for Britain in 1966. I knew how much it meant to him and I understood the setbacks he went through earlier in his career.

'Since coming back to live in Ireland, I'm certainly aware of some kind of antipathy. People say things in passing, and I think, "God, you're prejudiced," which is what they are. I find that jealousy and begrudgery are very much alive here, multiplied by two.

'My illness is progressive. I'm only too well aware that it will kill me. But, in the meantime, it's mind over matter sometimes, and I will screw up the courage to cross the floor when there is company here, and I maintain a certain decorum.

'When I'm here on my own I do occasionally dissolve in tears. It's a scary prospect to know that I'm not going to get better – only worse. And sometimes I look at him, and I wonder whether he realises it or not. He doesn't say much; if he did it might give the impression that he is weak and not able to cope. He is such a bundle of energy.

'My mind is the most important thing to me. If I can get my head around these things I'm laughing. I notice little things that I used to be able to do that I can't do any more. In the back of my mind is the wish that Hogan didn't have to put up with me. The thought of becoming a burden on him or anyone else is not at all pleasant.

'We did so much together when we first bought this place. We'd be out there weeding, cleaning, digging, planting and bedding in. Now I can't walk but there we are.

'It could be a lot worse. Oh yes, I'm not saying that lightly. My illness is not accompanied by pain of any sort, just sensations. I was reading about that great New Zealand athlete, John Walker, who also has Parkinson's. The only difference is that he has children and I do not. His courage is very obvious; you have to keep going as best you can and get your strength from somewhere else.'

11

My Best Race

The vast majority of people would tell you that my best race was winning the gold medal in Budapest. It was my biggest and greatest athletic moment without a doubt. But my most satisfying race was winning the Three-Mile Southern Championship of England on 19 June 1965. Two weeks before I had had a very bad run in the White City in the Inter-County Six-mile. I was leading after five miles (23 minutes 27.21 seconds), then suddenly I died. I came out of the race with two laps to go and I'm certain that I fell casualty to the heat. I was determined to atone for that in my next race.

Before the race I spoke to Gerry North, a Belgrave Harrier runner, and said, 'There's no point in hanging around waiting for these speed merchants. We'll make it between us. I'll take the first two laps, you take the next two, until we hit two miles.' He took the first two laps dead-on, I took over and we reached the mile in 4 minutes 21 seconds. There was no sign of Gerry, and they're all lined up behind me. I'm like an engine pulling the train. No one wants to take the lead.

Then quite quickly, a fellow I trained with came up and took over but he was only crawling along at seventy-one seconds a lap. By this stage I decided to take the initiative once and for all. Heading into the sixth lap I shot past him like a rocket and I got ten or fifteen metres away. My split for that lap was sixty-two seconds. I really blasted it for the next lap and then Mel Batty came out of the pack and reeled me in, clocking fifty-nine seconds. But I knew that was the finish of him. He had nothing left after that, and I kept the pedal down the whole way.

At two miles (8 minutes 59.2 seconds), I was about fifty metres in front and still driving hard. At the bell lap I was still fifty metres clear. I knew the pack was closing fast but I kept pushing, not knowing what was happening behind me now. I won by two seconds; I just held on and I was totally shattered. It was the only time I ran the second half of a three-mile faster than the first. I was chuffed at this tactical triumph and the negative splits. You see none of them would take the lead and my hand was forced. It was new territory for me as an athlete. I really hammered and thought, 'Now you'll run for it.' I got more satisfaction out of that race than any other I have run.

Those were prestigious events back in our day. Inter-county meets were regarded as being nearly as important as national championships so that's why there was always top-notch competition.

Rarely would you get an easy win; it might have seemed that way to the onlooker but you knew the quality of the opposition that was in the field. That was a big advantage to the athletes competing because sooner or later you would have to race against all of them.

There was no hiding, no skipping meets or changing distances at a championship. If you were good enough on the day you won. If you were beaten, you went away disappointed but determined to do better the next time. And because you were racing against quality athletes, defeat wasn't the end of the world. I learned to handle defeat in this way and it developed my racing mentality, which was a preference to be beaten by a good opponent than to win a meaningless race with no competition.

What happened to Gerry North and our race strategy? In fairness, Gerry wasn't in great form that day and wasn't able to do much to help me in that race. But let me tell you something about Gerry. I'm not sure he ever got the recognition he deserved. He was a brilliant cross-country runner and I don't know why but he always felt that he wasn't as good a track runner as his brother Geoff. They both ran for Belgrave Harriers.

He was a small fellow but he had a beautiful long striding action. Another thing I admired about him was his gutsy approach to running. He raced and raced; he could never get enough of racing and he never took the easy option. I remember one time he got a bad hamstring injury after a race. Usually that kind of injury is slow to heal, and nowadays athletes would take months off for that kind of injury. North was back training and racing in two weeks... two weeks!

Gerry was a brilliant soccer player as well. He was on the winning side for Blackpool FA Youth Club team against Leeds United, 4-2 at Elland Road. He played what they called outside-right in those days. Inside-right was George

Eastham, and also on that team was Jimmy Armfield. These were players who went on to become legends in English football. Gerry told me at the time that he did not think there was much money in football and also that he preferred an individual sport where he wasn't reliant on the rest of the team. He was right about the money part. That didn't come into football until much later. Football's loss was definitely athletics gain.

As an athlete, what I liked about Gerry was his belief in running to the front straight away in his races. He went flat out from the start and even if he got caught – as he sometimes did – he never changed the way he raced. David Bedford ran the same way, and that was my approach to racing as well.

12

The Toughest Athletes

Mohamed Gammoudi, Tunisia

I had a memorable but disappointing race against Gammoudi in the AAA six-mile Championships in the White City in the summer of 1965. I planned to make my move with two miles to go but it was raining all day. An hour before the race the rain stopped and I decided to run barefooted. After three laps the rain started again. When we reached the two-mile mark (9 minutes 13.4 seconds), I couldn't go as planned; it was too far out.

With three laps to go I hit for home and myself and Gammoudi went fifty yards away from the field. My legs started to slip on the track. I had no traction and got beaten for second place by two fellows who shot past me. I was only from here to the fireplace from the line and I should have been second to Gammoudi. We were well clear of the rest and we absolutely murdered them.

Gordon Pirie was my trainer at the time and he was shouting – 'You're clear. There is nobody there but Gammoudi.' The last lap was very frustrating because I was feeling great but not making any headway on the slippery cinders. All I could do was watch helplessly as Gammoudi moved further away. I don't know what the outcome would have been if the track was firm. All I had to show for my effort was a fourth place finish in 27 minutes 44.8 seconds.

We all knew about Gammoudi and his finishing kick. But that's athletics, a case of what might have been.

In the Mexico Olympics he ran away from Keino in the 5000-metre final to win the gold. A brilliant athlete, one of Africa's all-time greats in my opinion.

Mamo Wolde

Wolde started running because he wanted to be like his hero, Abebe Bikila. At one point they trained together at an airforce base in Ethiopia. He came into his own in Mexico when he won the marathon and finished second in the 10,000 metres. I used to meet Wolde when I was out training in Mexico. This was miles from the Olympic village out in quiet country areas.

I knew who he was because he had competed in Melbourne (1956) in the shorter distances, and he was in the Tokyo marathon although he failed to medal. His English wasn't great, but he immediately saw that I was running barefooted and he had this great big smile on his face. Wolde was a very quiet, serene kind of bloke. Like all the Africans I met during my career he was politeness itself, very reserved. We'd be the only two souls for miles around, no houses, roads, not much of anything. I got a strong sense that he respected me but he didn't have the words to say it. Years later I read that he had a horrible time of if, thrown into jail for life on a trumped-up charge in his own country. No man deserved to be treated like that. God help us but he'd have been better off if they'd shot him dead. It would have been kinder.

13

THE TOUGHEST COMPETITORS

I'm not hugely in favour of comparing athletes from different eras and distances. Generally speaking, all my competitors were tough and dedicated and made you work for the win. I have nothing but respect for those fellows I raced against in Britain and all over the world, and I'm also including the best of the Irish lads who ran in my time. With better facilities, support and competition, an awful lot of good Irish lads would have achieved so much more. They were talented and they had the mind for it, but you could only go so far in Ireland.

RON HILL

His record speaks for itself, doesn't it? He was the hardest man to beat in England when I was running. If you beat Hill, you'd nearly beat anybody. I don't know how he kept the motivation going for as long as he did. His best marathons have stood the test of time and would win a lot of races even in this era. He didn't have the high-tech equipment, sponsorship or any of that. Nor did he have access to all these high-powered minerals and vitamins. Mind you, I don't see much point in taking any of that stuff. It certainly won't make you a better athlete but I suppose for some it's a mental thing. Ultimately it's about hard graft, over and over, speed-work and commitment. Hill had all those and he was one hard man to race against.

Ron Clarke

Clarky was way ahead of them all. He was unbelievable, that man. I trained with him in Australia. He trained really hard and there was never an easy session. You went out the door and you were gone. He used to say: 'If you want to train with me we will go from the gun.' He might play squash with his brother for an hour and then run you ragged on a ten-mile run. I have spoken elsewhere about his misfortune that the Olympics were held in Mexico. Clever people who checked out the conditions there prior to the Olympics told me that European and Australian runners hadn't any chance at all. How right they were in his case. The Africans had an in-built advantage for coping with the altitude.

Derek Clayton

Ron Clarke was the best but the hardest trainer of them all was Derek Clayton. Clarke told me once that if you trained with Clayton every day for three weeks your career would be finished. Clarke couldn't take it. He trained with him once a week on a Sunday and that was enough for him. They'd run in the morning, and Clayton would go out again in the evening at about 4.00pm and do a twelve-miler inside an hour on his own..

To his credit, when he ran in Mexico, his knee was swollen

like a balloon. There was a cyst growing inside the cartilage. He finished sixth on pure guts.

He coached himself and that would have been in keeping with his attitude. I heard others say that he set out to create this image of himself as a bit of a mystery man. Mystery or not, he ran two incredible marathon races, setting a world record the first time and breaking it within two years. He became the first athlete to break the 2 hour 10 minute barrier, running a 2 minutes 9.36 seconds in Fukuoka in 1967. He then ran 2 minutes 8.33 seconds in Antwerp, Belgium in 1969. That record stood for more than twelve years.

Clayton said, 'Through miles and miles of training, I honed my leg action to such a degree that I barely lifted my leg off the ground.'

His one ambition in life was to beat Clarke over 10,000 metres. He trained at my place for about three weeks. The night before the race in Crystal Palace, they went to a hotel in London. They all got food poisoning and were very ill. Dick Taylor won the race. I finished in seventh position.

Clarke then took him with him to the Continent for a series of track meets and turned him into a complete zombie. After three or four days Clayton was gone. Clarke would run a 10,000 metres one night, jump on a plane for the 600-mile return, run a 5000-metre the next night, then go back again and run 3000 metres. Every day, five days a week, he could race, and he might run two world records in the week.

It was a disgrace what happened to him in Mexico. I've said it before and I'll never stop saying it. If the Olympics hadn't been held in Mexico, the gold medal was his in the

10,000 metres. He was still in it with three laps to go, and he was unconscious for three hours after the race was finished. I thought he was going to die. But by Jesus he still came out and qualified for the 5000 metres. That shows what he was made of.

TOM O'RIORDAN AND THE IRISH

Tom was an excellent runner. He never actually beat me. I remember overtaking him in a cross-country race up in Belfast. I also ran against him in Tralee. We did a three-mile time-trial in Santry stadium the morning we were due to fly out to Tokyo. He dropped out after two miles.

Bertie Messitt was another excellent runner. I remember beating him on a windy night in Santry. It was only after I retired that I got to know him. I have great time for Bertie; he's a lovely man and we keep in touch on a regular basis. He was definitely talented but unless you left Ireland in those days it was always going to be difficult.

You had Peter McArdle who ran for America, and Jim McNamara, another excellent runner. There were several others but because I was away in England for so long I lost touch with most of them.

14

'A Fearless Competitor': Athletes on Jim Hogan

Jim (JP) Reardon, Villanova and Ireland

A 1948 Olympian at 400 metres. Reardon was the first Irishman to attend Villanova University on an athletic scholarship, the original student-athlete. He paved the way for Ron Delany, Noel Carroll, Frank Murphy, Eamonn Coghlan and Marcus O'Sullivan, to name but a few.

'I read about Jim Hogan during my years in the States. I was interested in his story because he was born and reared near where my mother's people hailed from in Kilmallock. My mother was an O'Rourke, and I have many happy childhood memories of summers spent in and around Kilmallock with her relatives. First of all I'd like to know who gives a damn about whether he was Cregan or Hogan. He was a Limerick man, an Irishman for Chrissakes.

And as for running in a British vest, don't make me laugh. I fought in the Korean War for the Americans, and I'm proud that I did because I believed in what I was doing. I would have done the same thing if I was in Hogan's position. I sometimes wondered how different my athletic career would have been had I declared for America. It's a moot point for sure but I would have been in Helsinki in 1952.

Olympic athlete Jim Reardon.

'I remember a conversation I had with John Joe Barry about the troubles Hogan was having with the Irish officials. 'Nothing's changed in Ireland,' John said. 'The athlete is still the last person to be considered.' And he was dead right. Both John and I had high hopes of medalling in Helsinki in 1952, but the officials sent the tickets by boat and we got them a week after the games were over. Those same officials were still there in Hogan's time. They brought politics into it, and they were nothing but a bunch of little Napoleons.

'I don't think they ever broke a sweat, but it was their petty and punitive way of doing things that turned my stomach. Poor old John never ran again because of how they treated him. Yours truly got it in the neck as well, as did Hogan. And it was totally unnecessary. But it wasn't the athletes they hurt. They were really hurting Ireland. They were self-serving, clannish, and a detriment to athletics in the country.'

DAVID GUINEY (UNPUBLISHED INTERVIEW, NOVEMBER 1999)
David Guiney died within a year of giving this interview. He was a well-known sporting personality and journalist. He was also an outstanding athlete; he won an AAA title for the shot-put in 1948 and competed for Ireland in the Olympic Games in London that year. He was a sprinter and high jumper of note, but it was in the shot-put event that he made his name and broke the Irish record on several occasions.

Guiney, a former civil servant, became a sports journalist with the Irish Independent *and was then appointed sports editor of the* Irish Press. *Later he was the main Irish sports reporter for the* Daily Mirror, *and wrote innumerable books on sporting subjects as wide-*

ranging as golf, soccer, rugby and boxing, as well as his beloved athletics. He was the Irish authority on statistical information relating to the Olympic games, and he published several books on the Olympics over the course of a long career.

Many will remember Dave Guiney as being witty, funny and sarcastic. But he was always compassionate. This was very evident in his accomplished after-dinner speaking engagements. He had an in-built detector for hypocrisy and insincerity and was never afraid to ridicule it in his inimitable fashion. He was born in Kanturk, a proud Corkman, and never hesitated to allude to his origins. He died peacefully in Dublin in October 2000, aged seventy-nine, after a short illness.

'Who was this Jim Cregan/Jim Hogan? He came on to the marathon scene out of nowhere, or so it seemed to many.

'He collapsed at twenty-three miles and we saw him in the hospital after. He made a great remark to me which I've always talked about. He said to me, 'I didn't come here to make up the numbers. I came over here to try to win a medal and I did my best.' For twenty-three miles he ran step for step with Abebe Bikila, one of the all-time great marathon runners and unbeatable in his prime. Hogan ran himself to a standstill. He didn't give a damn about who his opponent was. He never did; that's not to say he didn't respect them because he certainly did. But it was all or nothing for him. You hear people talk about leaving it all out there in a match a race or whatever. Well, by Jesus, Hogan left it all on that course. He was totally dehydrated and he could have died out there.

'He was constantly fighting with the Irish officials, and they didn't like him. There was the mystery of the name Jim Hogan, and they weren't too sure or too pleased about that. To be fair they might reasonably have wondered which one he was and when did he leave one name behind and assume another. There may have been a breakdown in communication. Hogan most likely told them to fuck off and I can't fault him for that.

'He suddenly appeared on the Olympic scene in 1964. They couldn't find out his background or anything at all and he got on the wrong side of the Irish officials because he was looking for a few quid to help with his expenses. It wouldn't have been a whole pile of money. In any case these people basically wouldn't give you the itch then.

'Ah, he was treated badly without a doubt. He didn't help his cause but that was his way. He was a fiery devil. There wasn't much of a living for him in Ireland and he went to England and they certainly looked after him there.

'Where is he now, do you know? He's back in Ireland you tell me, in Knocklong? You must be joking? I'd love to meet that man again some day. Will you tell him I was asking for him? 'Twas a long time ago, lad.

'Was any of that helpful to you then? Come and see me when you're in Dublin, okay? Now bugger off.

'Cheers, lad.'

Tom O'Riordan, Irish Olympian 1964, 5000 metres

Tom O'Riordan is an unassuming and modest Kerryman. He was born in the village of Tubrid, about a mile from Ardfert. He had a remarkable athletic career and came to prominence after four hugely successful years on an athletic scholarship to Idaho State University, 1957–61. He competed in the 5000 metres in the 1964

Olympics and was leading the field in his semi-final before being overtaken with two laps remaining. He was also selected for the European Championships in Budapest in 1966, and clocked 4 minutes 2.8 seconds in the mile.

'I always found Jim to be very compatible and most friendly. He was an awful man to swear. He's still an awful man to swear! I suppose he was a bit wild but he was well respected in England. I always maintained that it was a pity he didn't get to run with us in the cross-country in Ostend in 1965. We had a very good team that year and he would have made it even better.

'He had a disagreement with Irish officials over the airfare and that definitely influenced his decision to make the break with Ireland. Having said that, money would have been fairly thin on the ground in those days and you had no great funding for athletics.

'He was a fearless competitor and of course he was only a handful, like a jockey, light as a feather. Even so he was wiry and very strong. I liked him; we got on fine, but he was working and training in Britain so he disappeared from the Irish scene.'

DONAL (DONIE) WALSH, LEEVALE AC, VILLANOVA, IRELAND
Donie Walsh, physiotherapist, coaches with Leevale AC. He is regarded as one of the shrewdest judges of talent not only in Ireland but in America. Marcus O'Sullivan (Head Athletics Coach, Villanova University) has no hesitation about asking Donie for advice on coaching schedules for the training of collegiate athletes. Walsh represented Ireland in the 1972 Olympic marathon but ran poorly due to an illness. He was a member of the Irish team that won the silver team cross-country medal in Limerick in 1979, when John

Treacy repeated as the individual gold medallist. Shortly after these championships Walsh discovered he had mumps before he toed the line in Greenpark Racecourse. He won a succession of national cross-country titles before retiring in the late 1970s.

'When I was coming through near the end of the 1960s, I suppose we all looked up to Ron Clarke. He was the king around that time. I ran against him once up in Dublin. I think it was in 1968. All I remember about that race was that he lapped me. Need I say any more?

'As regards the Irish athletic scene in those years, Jim Hogan would have been my hero, especially after he won the 1966 European marathon in Budapest. That was a brilliant achievement, wasn't it? I know he had several run-ins with the athletic governing bodies here and that but it was a disgrace that he had to declare for England. I thought we might be getting close to athletic unity in 1967 but it was a shame that people just didn't go along with it. I can't understand a government that would recognise three national governing bodies.

'It was later that I discovered I shared a birthday with Hogan, 28 May. He was the first Irishman in my era who really went out and did it. You had Noel Carroll as well but that was a different distance.

'I suppose the other thing about Hogan was that he wasn't gifted with pure speed. I could identify with that certainly and I won races that on paper I had no right to be winning. I'd say Hogan was a bit like that. You see there are loads of people with ability but they don't know how to win. The will to win can't be coached, and if you haven't the will to win you're wasting your time. Hogan was a fierce competitor altogether and he wasn't afraid of losing. You have to admire that in any athlete.'

FRANK GREALLY

Frank Greally was a member of the successful East Tennessee State University NCAA cross-country team in 1972. He has been editor of The Irish Runner *magazine for more than twenty-five years.*

'When I think of Jim Hogan, the words courage and commitment immediately spring to mind.

I think of Jim – an Irish warrior in a green singlet tracking the legendary Abebe Bikila for most of the distance in the Olympic marathon. I think too of Hogan, the runner's runner, coasting to victory in a British singlet in the marathon of the 1966 European Championships. It was his way of reminding Irish officialdom that he was a man of singular vision.

I think of him too as a self-made man of inner steel and a warm heart. He reminds me a lot of Dave Bedford, who came along years later to plough his own lonely furrow on the way to greatness. Jim Hogan was one of a rare breed that now seems to be almost an extinct species. He asserted his existence on this planet with passion and integrity and the Jim Hogan legend will endure.

JOHN CULLEN

John Cullen is a Wexford-born jump jockey

'I first got to know Jim Hogan over five years ago. I'm not sure exactly where we first met but it was at the races somewhere in Ireland. He was slight and he had the build of a jockey, and he was well known among the owners and trainers.

'As we got comfortable chatting I found that he had a fantastic understanding of horses, training and racing. He began to take an

Jim Hogan with jockey John Cullen at Thurles races. (Photo by Liam Healy.)

interest in me and as time passed he became very supportive.

'To be honest, I didn't have a clue about his achievements in athletics and he never drew it down either. It was only when I talked to others who knew him that I realised he was a world-class athlete in his time.

'One area that he knows more than most about is fitness: staying in shape and making weight. He would always encourage me to run, to put in a few miles, especially when I wasn't booked to ride. He kept saying that I needed to build up my stamina and that it would stand to me.

'I always did a bit of working out in the gym to strengthen various muscle groups. I hadn't paid a lot of attention to cardiovascular stuff. I would never have been much of a runner, I'd say.

'I will never forget the time when Jim took me out to a track for a light workout, as he called it. It was anything but light, I can assure you. He had me doing these laps, half-laps, at different speeds. The he'd let me jog for a bit and I'd do it all over again. I thought to myself, "This fella is trying to kill me."

'I was totally knackered when that session was over. Says he: "That was an easy interval workout today. We'll do this again in two days and you'll be motoring a lot harder." I was too tired to argue.

'Sure enough, the next day wasn't as bad, but I don't know if I was going harder or not. When it was done, Jim had the times, the rest phases and everything in a little notebook. He had me on the stopwatch all the time and never said a word.

'Gradually I began to understand the value of being physically strong and fit and also the necessity of having a strong endurance base. I talk to Jim a lot and sometimes he always asks me if I am running. "I just did a couple of laps around Baldoyle," I'd tell him, or whatever place was handy. He encouraged me to run on grass.

'When I got to know more about his athletic career, I was astonished at the mileage and training that he put in daily while holding down a full-time job. And there was no money in it for him. So in that respect he has been an inspiration to me – to persevere even when things aren't going all that great, just to keep at it and more than anything to stay in shape.

'He is an amazing man for his age and we have a great friendship that will go on no matter where my racing career takes me.'

15

The Lonely Breed

I was a great friend of Ron Clarke. He admired my style of running; like himself and indeed Dave Bedford, I ran from the front and didn't like runners who sat in. When he came to England to race, he'd ring me up and ask me to go to training in different places with him. We put in a lot of hours training together. Now I didn't even know at the time that he and Norman Harris were doing this book and Mary never said a word to me about it.

Norman Harris decided to include an chapter about me in his book, *The Lonely Breed*. His initial plan was to tell the story of an athlete who trained hard but didn't win the big one. During the writing of that chapter, I went out and won the gold medal in the European Championships. There was a bit of good-natured slagging about this of course, and they were forced to change the profile they had in mind.

I do think they made a very good job of it like. Ron Clarke and I are still close friends. I ring him up periodically. He was the unluckiest athlete ever born not to have won an Olympic medal. If the Olympics had not been held in Mexico in 1968 he would have had two gold medals – he was that good and that much better than anyone else in the world that year.

For the long-distance athletes accustomed to sea level, those Olympics were a complete waste of time.

Norman Harris was a frequent visitor to my house as he lived just up the road from us. And to be honest, they did have Mary down near-perfect, and she got on really well with them. Norman liked Mary and I think that was a big help to him in writing that chapter. Several people told me that they felt they knew Mary well after reading that chapter. Mary was also very pleased with what they wrote. She wouldn't have been boastful or going on about it; that wasn't her way ever. But you could tell that she was satisfied. Mary was a great reader and I think she appreciated what they were trying to get across.

After the book was published they sent me a copy. Wouldn't you know it, I gave it to somebody and I never got it back. Not too long after this, though, a friend of mine came to the door one night and said to me, 'I've got that book for you,' and he handed me a copy. I asked him how he managed to get his hands on it because it was not available in bookshops any more. 'Oh, I got it from a library,' he said, cool as you like. That was a quare few years ago now and I've managed to hold on to it. I've included the chapter about me in this book, beginning on page 123.

The book covers the whole spectrum of athletics, the highs and the lows, the elation and the heartbreak, the successful ones and those who fell just short. Ron and Norman wrote about some very accomplished athletes from that era and what I like best about it is how they showed that the difference between winning and losing is often times so difficult to explain.

That is why I would never label a good athlete who gives it all on the day and comes up short a failure. I get disgusted when I read ignorant comments in the papers by writers who know nothing at all about the sport. On any particular day good fortune, fate – call it what you like – decides who gets the medals. I'll never forget what was written about that poor guy Coghlan when he finished fourth in the Olympic final in 1976. And the stupid comments surrounding Sonia O'Sullivan after Atlanta. Coghlan was one stride from a gold medal. I trained with him (in New York) years later for the World Veterans' Championships, and I found him a super bloke, an absolute gentleman and a marvellous talent.

None of the athletes I competed against were failures or losers. That's a horrible and cruel label to put on any committed athlete. I see it happening all the time now and increasingly so. I think that's very sad.

16

'A Runner and His Wife'
from Ron Clarke and Norman Harris,
The Lonely Breed
(London: Pelham Books, 1967)

This was to be a chapter dedicated to the most typical of the breed – the trier. We thought that the story of Jim Hogan, which was a tale of dedication and of hope, would be a theme that could be recognised in any country where athletes train and train, look as though they are on the brink of great things, have predictions made as to the certainty of an imminent success, and then face some criticism and try again with even more dedication and determination. Most fail again and seem destined to remain on the brink of success. A few come through. And one of these was Jim Hogan. Most athletics followers know Jim's history. His favourite expression: 'You run until your eyeballs pop,' has a tinge of authenticity when he uses it. This is, then, a story of determination and what could happen if you have the guts of a Jim Hogan and the understanding and support of a wife like Mary. It's a story of what athletics is supposed to be all about and is – struggle.

***

He thought in terms of gold medals, of world records, of Number One. He was a top runner. That's the way he saw himself – even if others did not. No one else believed in him, except his wife.

Jim Hogan's life was entirely adjusted to running, and his wife's life to his. Jim worked as a groundsman, which suited his running; Mary, a university graduate, was private secretary to a publisher. One Sunday early in 1966 she sat in the front room of their flat, behind an anonymous doorway in a street in Chiswick, London, and discussed his running.

Said she: 'I think it's in Jim's character, myself. Whatever it is – it happens to be athletics – I think Jim would be more than usually dedicated to something he wanted. Or thought he ought to get. Or thought he could come by…'

'I want to run 13 minutes 10 seconds for three miles this year,' said Jim. 'I'd like a world record for thirty kilometres. The European marathon is the race I'd like to win.'

But it was not, explained Mary a question of Jim making a name for himself, not even a question of helping him to do the one thing that he could do better than anyone else…

'Yes,' said Jim. I am better at that than anything else…'

'It's not that,' she said. 'Not even because he's happy doing it. It's just that this happens to be what he believes in. He believes in what he's doing, he gives all he's got to it, and he takes the rough with the smooth…There's always something else you'd prefer to be doing, or you can think of a lot of other things you'd prefer. But you can't have it both ways. If you cut corners you don't get results. If you don't get results you're fed up…'

'Cut corners,' fired Jim, 'in yesterday's race!'

She pretended to punch him. They scrapped on the sofa. She escaped, laughing, and while he took out his training diary to enter up the week's mileage, she resumed the conversation.

She talked of being excited at seeing other people doing well, because of knowing what they put into it; and upset at seeing a good runner adrift in a race, because it ought not to be happening, being beaten by kipper herrings and so forth, and her thinking, 'How dreadful, take him away until he is fit again'; and of the satisfaction after one of Jim's wins, so there was that extra kick when he went out to train on the Monday and how by the end of the week it had slowly worn away and you were back to what you believed in and what you didn't believe in. That was how it had been all along, that was how it had to be: a lot of rough with the smooth. If it was just coming his way without him putting a lot of effort they would probably go and do something else. She never actually used the words 'triumph' and 'struggle' or the name of Baron de Coubertin…

Jim was puzzling aloud over Tuesday's evening run. It arrested her attention.

'You did go out in the evening,' she said, 'because you were in at about a quarter to six.'

He: 'B'Jasus, that's the evening I did…'

She: 'You ran around the…'

He: 'I ran around my circuit.'

She: 'The Richmond circuit.'

'Yes,' said both of them.

Behind that Chiswick doorway, Jim Hogan was a secure

man. Outside it, he was almost completely alone. No one else had much faith. And he did not work very hard to get it.

His real name of Cregan he had left behind when he departed County Limerick, Ireland. He had in other ways burnt the bridge back to Éire. He had said he did not want to run for them any more, that there was nothing there for him, they had only sent him somewhere when they could not avoid it. And in London he had not tried very hard to win friends among club mates. He ran only when he wished, not as a 'club man'. He delighted in rubbing in his superiority to lesser club runners.' Look, Trevor,' he'd say before a club race. 'There's only one thing wrong with me and that is I can't understand why I go up to the park to race against you because, Trevor, I know I'm going to beat you by two-and-a-half minutes in half an hour's time.'

He preferred to be left to himself as a groundsman, because then he could grab opportunities to train. He was prepared to run in little circles around a concrete-floored shed, keeping an eye open for his foreman, for half an hour.

Mainly he was on his own because of a label for unreliability. Representing Éire, he had not finished in any of the 5000 and 10,000 metres in the 1962 European Championships, and the 10,000 metres and marathon in the Tokyo Olympics. He had once pulled out of a six-mile championship a few laps from the finish when in the lead. His main justification for this 'coming out', as he always referred to it, was that he was interested only in number one position. In the Tokyo marathon he claimed he had ran a true race by challenging Bikila, until crumbling at the twenty-three-mile mark. But some people said that he had only been ensuring that he got some of the spotlight, some cheap glory. This made him furious, but there was nothing he could do. Scarcely a single journalist was prepared to give him publicity. He had no name, no position, to force others to listen.

He was regarded suspiciously in official and selectorial circles, and he did not try to use his Irishman's tongue in an effort to charm these important people. He had finished third in the 1966 British Cross-Country Championships, but nobody had pressed very hard to gain his inclusion in the English team for the international event. He had broken the British 10,000 metres record the previous track season, without gaining selection for Britain in an international match.

Other runners could not accept him on any common level. He was neither a champion who was beating them, nor a second-rater to whom they were superior. He was likely to lead them by half a lap all the way in a six-mile before 'blowing up' at five miles. Afterwards he would say of them that they had not run like real runners should, staying in a bunch like that half a mile back. They would say that in fact *they* had, that they'd judged and spread their effort evenly, and it was he who had not run like a real runner should. But it was tentative, uneasy criticism. They were not able, like the journalists, to ignore him. They knew that he was tough and he had ability, a man who any day might trash them.

He knew it too. But the proof was so elusive. He would run a tremendous solo trial on grass track amidst a high wind, run his best time – and then end up, after the all-important race a few days later, asking himself why he had not managed even to repeat that time. He did not have much patience with himself: he was fairly used to being disillusioned. He began to take refuge in the fame of what he almost did. He took it out in other solo trials, in training, in races against club mates and with incredible club records. He found himself running so much better when he did not expect to, or have to. For example, the day after he was married, when he had been at hospital all night with his wife ill, and she persuaded him to go along anyway to the race; sleepless, and sure that he would not run well, he ran his fastest mile – and two days later his fastest six miles. What was much tougher was the onus of having to run well, of having to run as well as he believed he could, but never had…His biggest requirement was confidence. What he needed most was an ordinary performance, an unspectacular, solid foundation stone.

If it wasn't for his life behind the doorway in the Chiswick street, Jim Hogan would have been very much alone. But every night when he was out training, Mary was at home preparing the evening meal and hoping that the run was going well. They both knew that the label of a non-finisher was something that had to be overcome, regardless of any philosophy about number-one-or-nothing. He had to finish each time, no matter what humiliation it might mean. To that extent he would pander to the public opinion and officialdom. They would both pander.

By the summer season of 1966 Jim Hogan had been a consistent finisher for many months, without being accepted.

His immediate target was the British marathon championship.

He knew from his Olympic run against Bikila that he obviously had great potential for the event. In Tokyo he had gone through thirty kilometres in better than world-record time for that distance. He had done no special marathon training then; the pounding from the hard road had been his destruction, not the pace. He was now an international-class track runner, capable of running at a lively pace but handicapped by an absence of finishing power. However his overall speed, his brisk, short-stepping action, his lack of weight, ought to make him an ideal marathon man. And along with that the courage, the guts that he was only too keen to demonstrate. All he needed was real confidence instead of the hope he called optimism.

He decided to have a run over the course on which the British marathon was to be held, from Windsor to Chiswick. He had counted on getting someone to accompany him in a car and check the course. When, at the last minute, nobody could be found, he was quite upset. But he wanted to carry on. The 'run over the course' had become very important. He wanted to see that he could run without stopping, efficiently, for twenty-six miles. He went to Windsor by train. His clothes were taken back by a young Canadian. He went off course early on, cursing and almost in tears when he realised his mistake. He finally completed an estimated twenty-six miles, in reasonable time. He was then seven miles short of the finish on the course proper. He was given a partial lift to Chiswick in the back of a carpenter's van, and then, cold and stiff, hobbled two-and-a-half miles to pick up his clothes. It was the sort of 'long run' made by youths fired with the challenge of being distance runners. Jim Hogan, thirty-three years old, was possibly just as pleased at having completed the distance.

Two months later he ran in the British marathon. One enthusiast told him he could run two hours and ten minutes, the world's fastest time. Others told him just to finish. Half an hour before the start of the race he was urged: 'You're not going to impress anyone if you don't finish; even just crawling half-way down the field, you're going to win a lot of admirers.' He was too nervous to take much notice. 'I know,' he muttered. 'I know.' He already knew what he had to do.

On a hot, humid day, the opening pace was very slow. He let others dictate it and then, around fifteen miles, went away with young Brian Taylor. Anxiously, he ran with Taylor past twenty miles and on to the stadium…It was only after they had got to the stadium, and he had been left standing by Taylor's lightning last lap, and had finished, that he realised that there had been nothing like the strain he had feared. It had really been quite an easy run. Perhaps he could have won it if he'd gone hard from twenty miles. But second wasn't really so bad. He knew it was true when other people said to him that this was exactly the sort of run that he needed. Now he had it behind him; now he knew what he could do. Also, he had ensured his first selection for Britain – for the marathon at the European championship in Budapest.

He did more training on road surfaces. In early August, one month before the European championships, he raced in Finland. He won at 10,000 metres and 5000 metres. They were his first wins in international competition. In the weeks before departing for the games he ran an undulating fifteen-mile road course on which his best time had been seventy-eight minutes; he did seventy-five minutes, which was world-class running. He was very quickly starting to realise that he was in great form; and it was a strange feeling, this confidence he was now aware of. On the eve of the departure Mary Hogan was told by a doctor that her health, which had worried both of them for some time, appeared to be much better.

Every day he ran he felt good. On the first day in Budapest, a week before the race, he ran a few easy miles with the other distance runners. They told him he was running fast. The next day he ran five miles with the other Irishman, Derek Graham. Graham said he'd never run so fast in training. To himself it didn't feel fast. He ran two miles with the miler Alan Simpson, running freely along roads and country pathways. 'You're the fittest man in the camp,' said Simpson.

'Sure I hope so,' said Hogan.

Said Simpson: 'Run with them for eighteen miles, then go. You'll leave them for dead.'

Said Hogan: 'That's the way I'm going to.'

He'd been thinking more about how he might have won the British marathon, how he must run this one. Calculatingly. Not in the way he ran most of those six-mile races – eyeballs-out from the start, regardless of the world-record pace, and then disappointed at finally cracking up. But in the way that other runners, like milers, won track races – with a comfortable pace for three-quarters of the journey and then a fast finish. It wasn't possible for him in track race, he did not have real speed, but in a marathon…He told himself that he should not cooperate in any early move, that he would go with the move only if it was made by someone really good.

In training he was finding it hard to hold himself back, but he knew he had to. He ran with others who he knew would ensure it. Outside of training it was more difficult to retain himself. He seized hold of the gold medal won by Lynn Davies in the long jump. 'Give me a good look at that,' he said. 'I'll be winning on Sunday.'

Almost every day a team official said to him: 'Remember, Jim. Just finish.'

Finally he replied: 'Sure I'll finish, First.'

Most took these as sure signs of nervousness, or the impulsive comments of an erratic Irishman who always had to be different. Not many were aware that he was in fact feeling confident – or, at least, very excited by the realisation that he was in the form to win.

It was something of a surprise to him that he was feeling like this, and that he slept soundly on Saturday night, and felt good as he ate his cereal and sultanas, drank his well-sugared tea on race morning – feeling good within himself, excited but not desperately nervous.

At three o'clock in the afternoon, when he went to the mark in the Nepstadion to run for the first time for Britain, he was distinctively himself. His shorts, which had been acquired from an Oslo store, were red with white trimming. He had worn them for twelve months; they were, in effect, his own colours. The Union Jack on his vest was hidden by the race number which had been pinned dead-centre over his chest. On his feet were the lightest, thinnest-soled road shoes manufactured, made even lighter by the triangular holes he'd cut all over the top.

After resting a great deal in the previous two or three days and eating well, he had been troubled by a cramp when warming up. So he did a lot of stretching exercises and jogged for twenty-five minutes. Now he felt ready to go.

Drawn on the outside of the bunch, he went fast out and shot across. He went close up to the front then settled in. It was easy, he could not feel his feet. Now all he had to do was to be patient. As long as he did not have any difficult decisions to make, as long as the pace was not too slow…

Out of the stadium, on the road, a Pole had gone away by fifty yards. But no further, and it not even seem to be a matter for debate. The pace did not seem to be slow, and the Pole was not going any further away. They ran in a clockwise circle and came back past the stadium. A big special clock showed they had done about sixteen and a half minutes for the first five kilometres. That meant roughly fifteen and three quarter minutes for the three miles. Reasonable. Not fast but not slow. The Pole had come back to them.

Hogan looked around at the rest of the bunch and saw it contained about twenty. It seemed a little surprising to him, strange, the way he was able to look at the others. As if he was sitting in a chair, waiting for something to happen…

The road was flat, almost dead-flat. Some parts were cobbled, in others the tarmac was uneven, and sometimes there was a tram line. He was quite happy to negotiate it all, to take in everything, to get at least to the turn before preparing for action. Toth of Hungary and Perez of Spain were forcing and going ahead. Perhaps if he'd felt more anxious, even a fraction more anxious, he'd have gone with them. But he was happy to keep them within range, fifty yards up the road. He was running easily enough to move straight up to them if he wanted to. If they were still out there at the turn he would go up.

They were in the country now, on better roads. The afternoon was warm but he wasn't perspiring badly. Sometimes he dabbed the perspiration away from his wrists. The inside of the wrists, so they said, was where the circulatory system was most quickly heated or cooled, which was why some of the others wore wrist bandages. He was careful to apply the cold sponge water to his wrists. Otherwise he didn't need a sponge. He wondered how long he was going to keep feeling good like this.

Eventually Toth and Perez drifted back to the bunch, without any obvious change in pace. It was still pretty much as it was in the start: the five-kilometre times were confirming that.

By the time they came to the turn they were already past half-way, because of the five-mile starting loop, and the turn seemed to become a very important point indeed in the race. It was possible to sense a real urgency among the bunch as they came up to it. They turned in a village square, with the whole village out to watch. There was patriotic cheering for Toth. Hogan, cornering well on the tight turn, found himself ahead. In the lead. But only briefly. Toth grabbed it back…

Suddenly something had happened to the race. They were no longer just running along. In front, Toth was pushing hard.

Faces had come up close one either side, they were three or four abreast. He sensed that were not any others with them, that they numbered only about five. But he did not look around. He felt good. He could hear the deep breathing and hard blowing all around him, and his own breath was fine. The only thing was his feet – he'd felt the blisters growing for the last half-hour. But blisters could be disregarded, blisters were nothing. It was like a pain-killing drug, the way the rest of him felt good.

Now Toth was moving away by a fraction. So Hogan went up to him. Twice more Toth moved away and came back. 'By God,' said Hogan to himself. 'He's trying to surge.' And to realise that, and to hear Toth blowing, and to know that he was running within himself, made him feel very good indeed.

They came up towards the thirty-kilometre mark. Nearly nineteen miles, seven-and-a-half to go. The refreshment point appeared. But he did not need a drink. The others swung aside for theirs. They must have all gone across, he was on his own. He was in the lead. He began to feel like the leader. He kept on for a mile, waiting to see if they were going to close up. He guessed the gap at about thirty yards. But they did not close up. He was very definitely the leader. This was it. He went harder…and was instantly surprised at how much faster he suddenly was running. He was running strongly. And it was rather frightening too, because now his cards were on the table. He had opened up until he hit 'ceiling' pace, and now he knew what it was, and all he could do was try to hold to it and hope no one could run faster. He did not look around.

He was not going to look around, not once.

The thirty-five-kilometre mark came up. This time he could do with a drink to sustain him for the finish, four miles away. He did not dare slacken, and as he reached out with is hand he knocked the cup and it fell to the ground. But there were sponges up the road – that was all he wanted, water over his head. It was good, in a way, that he had not been tempted to ease off and drink. Perhaps the others would do that again and lose more time.

This was the tough part. This is where he would win if he was going to. He couldn't go any faster but he shouldn't need to. Just by holding on to this pace he would surely stay clear. It was faster than at any other stage of the race, that was certain. He saw, on the other side of the road, the ten-kilometre mark for the outward journey. And that meant – with the opening loop and the five-kilometre mark outside of the stadium – and five from ten was five – five more kilometres to the stadium. Three miles or near enough. What was three miles? Coming over Hammersmith Bridge, on the Richmond circuit, with three miles left to Chiswick. 'No trouble when you're on Hammersmith Bridge, boy…And while you were thinking that you've run further. Inside three miles now.'

'You're going great, Jim!' came a voice. 'But Vandendriessche is coming through.'

A left turn presented a long straight, maybe a two-mile straight, with apartment blocks down either side. And no traffic, except the station-wagon leading the way. He kept watching the back of the station wagon and the long empty straight on either side of it.

'You're still going well, boy,' he was saying to himself. 'You're still running faster than you were before you took off. Anyone who catches you will have to be running faster. You're tired but they're more tired…This straight – you're coming from the Hammersmith fly-over down there and you ended up running 1 hour 15 minutes for fifteen miles. You feel great down there at night passing all the traffic queued up. It feels worse here, that's all. But you're still running well, boy…You always said, Number One is all that counts, and every other time it was nowhere, and now the first time it's anywhere, it's Number One. You always said if it was the gold you were running for, then you would finish even if you were out on your feet…'

The long straight had ended, the stadium had come into sight. Crowds were on either side of the road. He was not looking at the people or any longer at the back of the leading car. He was watching the flags on the top of the stadium. They were getting very close. He had not ever looked back.

He heard the voice of Charlie Dibbs of Belgrave Harriers. 'Hogan, it's in the bag! There's no one in sight!'

He'd be inside in a minute, and then there would be no stopping him.

He swung down into the entrance. It felt good, rolling off the slope and swinging right on to the outside lane of the track. It was not difficult now, he could force himself more if he wanted to. But he just kept running steadily, not moving his head an inch, getting satisfaction from the efficient rhythm… Until he had broken the tape. And then the tiredness and the anxiety suddenly fled. He ran on towards the shouting English contingent in the stand. Then he ran into the centre of the ground and did what Bikila had done at Rome: calisthenics, 'bicycle-pedalling'. He felt tremendous. He waved and blew kisses around the arena. He had already looked back – for the first time – and seen no one else inside on the track. Now, as they began coming in, he started running up and down the straight to watch them finish.

They were finishing well, and he knew that he had out-paced them. From thirty kilometres onward he had in fact maintained a speed greater than at any previous point. For five kilometres they had almost stayed with him but had then faded in the next five. The race had been run, and won, like a mile race.

While Jim was waving to every single person in the crowd at the Nepstadion, Mary was at home by herself in the front room of the Chiswick flat, knitting and watching the television. She watched from the corner of one eye while she knitted. She was glad but not excited. It was not that she believed it would happen. But…the struggle of each day of the previous weeks and months and years had already passed, and that was the important thing.

17

HORSES AND HEROES

I got into horses at an early age and I never lost my passion for racing, training, breeding and riding out. It was inevitable that horses would be a big part of my life. You could say it was in the blood. My father used to buy yearlings and break them; mind you they were only working-class horses. He bought two or three a year and he was very good at it. He had a great sense or intuition about the animals and that rubbed off on me. I was very young at the time and my outstanding memory is that he had only the one failure in his whole career, a horse that kept running away that he couldn't control. I'd say that's not a bad return from a lifetime in the business.

I got into the serious end of the sport when I went to work for Joe Hogan (no relation). I started working with racehorses and over the next three years I learned an awful lot. We had some nice horses and a few good winners. There was a lovely mare called Come Again that won a bumper in Listowel.

We had another one called Waterscape owned by a Mrs King. She won a bumper in Clonmel and later notched the winning bumper in Listowel. Joe was in the saddle and he was a brilliant rider. I learned by watching Joe: how he handled horses before, during and after races, things like running off the pace, finding strides, but more than anything how he got the very best out of a horse.

He could win on horses that had no right to win. That's what a true horseman can do; that's what the best jockeys do. I don't know if it can be taught. I'd say in many cases it's a gift. One of the things he taught me was to respect but not fear the animal. You have to adjust to the horse because each one is an individual and very intelligent.

In 1959, I decided to leave the horse side of the game and went to England. Countless others took the same path; it was a bleak time in County Limerick as far as jobs were concerned. We had no education beyond primary level so there was no option. I lived in England for thirty-five years and I never rode horses during that time. Of course I was still passionate about horses and racing but my job and my athletic career took up quite a lot of my time, especially at weekends. I attended race meetings whenever I could.

When I returned to Ireland with my wife Mary, almost inevitably I got involved again. Physically I was in excellent shape after my athletic career and I always managed to get out for a run whenever possible. Consequently, I never gained or lost any weight. At various times I started riding out for Austin Leahy, Gerry O'Neill, Fran Costelloe and John Gleeson. Riding out was satisfying but I wanted something more, a bit of a challenge if you like. That was when I decided to start breaking horses for people and doing horses for the sales. This was a new experience for me and I learnt quite a lot about horses and their moods and tendencies, much the same as you would with a person.

By 2004, I'd had twenty-four horses leave the yard and they'd all won. I must say I was very, very lucky in that respect. It was only a matter of time before I took the next step and got into horses of my own.

First Down Jets was one of the first horses that I bought and then sold on to Liam Burke. He had won maybe two or three point-to-point races and he was quite a good horse. His most noteworthy success came in the 2006 Foxhunters' Championship Chase (three miles two furlongs) where he was second by a length to Why So Mayo. Conor Sweeney was on board that day and he was returned at 66/1. I didn't have a bet on him, however.

Now I have a few horses of my own. I had a nice chestnut horse by Flying Legend and My Native Mare, called Marathon Jim. He had one run in a point-to-point last year and finished fourth but unfortunately he died because of a heart problem.

The other horse is a nicely-bred grey mare by Environment Friend. She's shaping up well and has just run her first point-to-point. I also have a three-year-old by Close Conflict. My yard is small and tidy, with plenty of room to gallop and good grass.

Training horses a serious venture and can become very expensive when an animal breaks down or gets sick. It's as much a hobby as anything else. Relatively speaking, I turned out a good number of winners; with the exception of two, all my horses won races. That's the positive, exhilarating end of it.

But there is another side to the game too. I had two horses

that won twelve races between them and they both got killed. This was unfortunate because they still hadn't reached their best. So you're looking at a loss of earnings. But that's not the worst of it. To watch an animal get killed is beyond words really but it does happen. I don't know anybody who isn't moved by that. But it is part and parcel of racing; you just hope it doesn't happen too often. I don't expect I'll get rich from racing; that's not why I am involved in it. For me, money couldn't buy the satisfaction that comes from being around these animals.

Outside The Rails

I've been to Cheltenham every year since 1960. If you follow National Hunt racing the annual Cheltenham Festival is the place to be. I saw all the big winners going back to the time of the legendary Arkle and Millhouse. I like a gamble but I never get carried away. The fun goes out of it if you go down that road.

Jumping, chasing is my first love really but I follow flat racing as well. I went to Michael Stoute's yard when he had Shergar. He was a magnificent horse and what happened to him was very sad. I know quite a few flat jockeys, but I don't go to flat races a lot.

I go to as many race meetings as I can. That would include all the main venues in the south: Limerick, Cork, Galway, Leopardstown, Listowel – you name it. Once I even drove to Downpatrick and back.

When I stopped running in 1970, I had more time to attend racing and got to know some very good racing people.

I had two or three genuine friends, and one of these was John Buckingham. He rode a winner in the Grand National, and he was quite a good jockey. More than anything else though, he was a lovely, lovely, man.

Every year they held a cricket match between the jockeys and the valets and I used to do a charity run for them on the cricket pitch. I got to know a lot of the lads because of my involvement in this, some of the top jockeys like Warren Marsden and Richard Dunwoodie. I never talked shop to them about horses or racing; we got to know each other as people on a friendly basis and you'd see a completely different side to them away from the racing environment.

I will never forget the heated battler between Dunwoodie and Adrian Maguire for the jockey's title. It was hyped up in the press no end and it came down to the last day. I know that when all is said and done these lads never hated each other. They drove each other relentlessly and of course there were flare-ups, but the mutual respect is always there.

I think that is why jockeys are so totally different from other athletes. There is a camaraderie among them that the punter could never understand. I saw it myself but I wasn't part of it. They know that it can all go wrong in any given race: a horse breaks a leg and gets destroyed; and even worse a jockey gets a bad fall, a fatal tumble or a career-ending one. I have witnessed at first-hand the heartbreak and the devastation, the premature ending to a great career.

DECLAN MURPHY

In the late spring of 1994, Ireland was in the grip of World Cup fever. Jack Charlton and the Irish team had qualified for the 1994 finals, which were to be held in America. I'm not a big football fan but I admired Charlton and the whole country was caught up in it. A tragic racing accident took place during that time and it ended any interest I had in Ireland's performance.

My best friend over the jumps in England was Declan Murphy. He grew up in Hospital, County Limerick, a few miles from my place. For two years I drove Declan to all his races. As you can imagine, this took us to every course in Britain many times over. I drove him to Haydock on the day his career ended in a fall that could have killed him.

He was riding a horse called Arcot for Jeremy Glover. The horse had fallen before with Declan. Coming to the last fence, he was in third or fourth position, running a good race and gathering himself for the run-in. The horse crashed to the ground and Declan was flung off. Charlie Swan was behind Declan going over the last fence and his horse kicked Declan on the head as he went past. It happened in an instant, a freak thing, and I immediately rushed to Declan. I got down to the last fence and fifty yards away I could hear him breathing. He was lying there unconscious, in a terrible state.

We rushed him to a small local hospital and from there he was taken to hospital in Liverpool. There was nothing for me to do but follow on and wait. I stayed overnight in the hospital, sitting in the Admissions area, unable to sleep, pacing back and forth, not knowing what was going to happen. Luckily for Declan the top trauma surgeon was there that evening. They performed emergency surgery to remove a blood clot from his brain. His skull was fractured in several places and his jaw was broken.

He was still unconscious one week later; he hadn't recovered or made any real progress.

He looked frightful, battered and bruised, with tubes and monitors all over the place. I looked at him and I thought, 'Declan will be very lucky if he lives through this.' To be honest I wasn't very hopeful at that point, and I wondered what kind of condition he'd be in if he lived. I thought about his family back in Limerick, people I knew well. It was a dark, dark, time for me.

At the time of the fall he had been moving house and I was doing some work for him. I went back to that, trying to stay busy, to keep myself occupied. The doctors, nurses and all the staff at the hospital were brilliant. He regained consciousness and began a long and arduous rehabilitation. He had to learn how to walk again and it must have been terribly frustrating for him. To be fair, though, he did exactly what the surgeons told him to do, and during the rehab not once did he not cooperate. Eventually he did start to walk and his recovery continued. I never saw a man so determined to get better. His recovery was amazing.

Seventeen months later, on 10 October 1995, he was back on a racehorse. Not only was he back, he won the Annual Flat and Jump Jockeys' Challenge on a horse called Jibereen.

His professional riding career was over but it was important for him to get back in the saddle and prove something to himself.

It was a dramatic and emotional return and it showed how well he had recovered. He got his life back. His improvement continued to the point where he no longer takes medication. He can drive and he can still ride out in the morning. I went to his wedding in Spain last year. He may go to live there permanently. No matter what he does with his life our close friendship will always remain.

People sometimes ask me how I rate him as a jockey and so on. I have little time for this kind of analysis either for Declan or in my own athletic career. What I remember most about him was his ability to hold a horse up until about the last fifty yards in a race, and then produce him and win. He was special; he had something else. His win in the Two Mile Champion Chase in Cheltenham (1993) on Deep Sensation (trained by Josh Gifford) was textbook stuff.

The influence of P.P. Hogan was a huge factor in Declan's formative years. Declan has two brothers, Pat and Eamon, both jockeys. Eamon worked for Josh Gifford as second jockey behind Declan. He was very good in his own right. Pat rode in Ireland for years but had retired from riding when I got to know him. All three got started with P.P. as youngsters in Ireland.

They lived near P.P's and they'd go there before and after school. That's where they learned how to ride. P.P. made three good jockeys out of them. He's legendary, of course, for the advice he gave John Magnier, Robert Sangster and many more. He is gifted when it comes to selecting and buying potential winners. But his knowledge of riding and showing youngsters the ropes is unrivalled.

I've been around horses all my life but I knew I didn't have what it takes to be the best as a jump jockey. I didn't want to be a mediocre no-name so I turned to athletics. Even so, I always had an ambition to ride in a competitive race. Three years ago I got a chance in a charity race in Mallow, thanks to my friend Austin Leahy. He entered two horses for the race. The horse I was supposed to ride went lame the day before but Austin switched me on to the other horse, which I had never ridden.

Twenty-one runners went to the start, and Austin's one piece of advice to me was, 'Stick to the rails the whole way round.' I followed his instructions as best I could and I finished in ninth, which wasn't too bad. More important to me was getting an opportunity to go out there and test myself: Austin gave me that. I'm not sure the officials were too impressed and they put a ban on me, declaring that nobody over fifty-six could ride in charity races any more. I was seventy-one. That was the end of my charity racing.

18

FINAL THOUGHTS

I liked running and racing provided I was doing it well. I never liked being beaten by blokes that I knew I could beat if I were running at my best. I didn't mind getting my arse kicked by good blokes who were running within a couple of seconds of my best time ever, but I wouldn't have been satisfied with losing to fellows running 13 minutes 50 seconds and 13 minutes 55. I just couldn't take that. I suppose it has to do with the competitive instinct. I would rather be beaten in a fast race by class runners where I was taken to the limit than win an event in a mediocre time. There was no satisfaction in that, no challenge or sense of achievement.

What I liked best in athletics was the feeling I had when I was running well. I think that's true of any committed athlete. I liked the travelling, mind you, and athletics took me to twenty-five different countries. The blokes I mixed with and competed against were good blokes – 99 per cent of them anyway.

It's a great thing to be born with speed: you're half-way there. All you have to do then is work. If I had a sprint finish, I'd have won a lot more races, and that's a fact. If I could have run a last lap in fifty-six or fifty-seven seconds I'd have been fantastic.

Jim Hogan in the Tokyo Olympics (1964) Irish blazer.

In my younger days in Ireland I had no idols to look up to. I admired Gordon Pirie because he was a fantastic runner. The reason he was great was because he trained three times harder than anybody else. Emile Zatopek was doing the same thing in his era, and he would put himself through 40x400-metre intervals of speed work. That's ten miles, any way you cut it, and I don't know if any other athletes had the will to approach those distances. And look at Jim Alder. He had no speed and he still turned out to be a great runner through sheer hard work and training.

Most of the white runners have given up and left it to the Africans. The training is better; the shoes are better; the 10,000 metres has gone soft because they're using sponges on the track. I never thought we'd see that. They still talk about climate. It shouldn't enter into it now as athletes can go and train at altitude and in warm weather. And they're still whingeing. There was a Belgian runner a few years ago who wouldn't run a marathon if the temperature was over 65°F.

There's nothing in Ireland at the moment when it comes to distance runners. The same in England; all they have is sprinters. What has happened to create this mediocrity? When we were running there were ten of us under the qualifying times. We had ten inside twenty-eight minutes for the six miles in the White City. I put it down to hard work. We didn't have the comforts. I ran the fastest time in the world for six miles in Paddington after putting in a day's work. They've got it too easy now. The Africans do work and that's why they are getting the results.

That's why Sonia was so successful and such a marvellous

athlete. She trained with people who were better than her. As a track runner she was a sight to behold: she was graceful, smooth and balanced, and she knew how to win.

Now the clock dictates everything. It's all running against the clock. We ran against individuals who made us better competitors, and in that way we learned how to race. You can't run against the clock and not run against an individual. If you go out to win all the time, the times will fall automatically.

I'm not too pleased by some of what I see at present. I think the agents have too much influence in the sport and should be run out of it. They're good for the top athletes but no good for the sport. They're only catering to an elite minority of the athletes and they're on 10 per cent commission, 10 per cent expenses. I think that's bad for the sport. All you see at the Grand Prix meets are these pacemakers for the top runners. They get paid to do a couple of fast laps or miles and then come off the track. That does my head in. I don't mind a bloke winning big money, more luck to him. But if you're good enough to go out and set a world record, you ought to go out and do it on your own – go out and run a world record.

The times are over-emphasised now. People used to travel to see races, to watch lads trying to beat each other, to enjoy the competition. If you went to a local sports meeting all you wanted to see was a local lad winning a race or giving it a go. I'm telling you there's nothing better than to see a bunch of fellows all going for the win. That's what racing is all about. Go and watch athletes running to win for their clubs, no clocks, no pacemakers – that's the essence of the sport. I couldn't tell you what the world record is for any of

Titles Which I Have Won.

EUROPEAN MARATHON CHAMPION. 1966

6 mile INTER Co. and BRITISH GAMES CHAMPION 1963

SOUTHERN Co. 6 mile CHAMPION 1965 and 1966

SOUTHERN Co 3 mile CHAMPION 1965.

HOLDER of 12 IRISH CHAMPIONSHIPS, FROM 2 mile to 10 mile

HOLDER of 7. Middlesex CHAMPIONSHIPS

HOLDER of 18 13 IRISH COUNTY CHAMPIONSHIPS

HOLDER of 11. SOUTHERN IRISH CHAMPIONSHIPS

HOLDER of 18. POLYTECHNIC CLUB CHAMPIONSHIPS

NORTH of THE THAMES CROSS Country CHAMPION 1963

HOLDER of 4. LONDON CHAMPIONSHIPS

HOLDER of 2. INSURANCE CHAMPIONSHIPS.

HOLDER of 4 WALTON CLUB CHAMPIONSHIPS.

Records Which I Have Held or Still Hold.

		HOUR	MINS	SECS
30,000 METRES WORLD RECORD		1	32	25.4

	MIN	SEC		MIN	SEC
MIDDLESEX 3 and 6 mile RECORD.	13	19.6		27	33

		MIN	SEC
EUROPEAN 3 miles INDOOR RECORD		13	37

IRISH RECORDS, 3 6 mile 10,000 metres, 1 HOUR, 10 miles 5 mile 4 mile

POLYTECHNIC CLUB RECORDS. 2. 3. 4 and 6 mile 10,000 Metres 1 HOUR, 10 mile 15 mile metres 20,000 metres 25,000 30,000 metres WALTON CLUB Record 5 7½ and 9 mile Cross Country and MARATHON

ROAD RELAY RECORDS. 10. TRACK RECORDS 23. 61

Above and facing, Jim Hogan's own record
of athletics titles he won and records he held.

SOUTHERN CHAMPS	3	W	1
IRISH CHAMPS	12.	N	
COUNTY IRISH	18	2	
COUNTY ENGLISH	7	1	
SOUTHERN IRISH	11	2	
~~County IRISH~~			
POLY. CLUP. CHPS	18		
NORTH of THAMES. CHPS	1	1	
LONDON CHPS	4	1	
INSURANCE CHPS.	2	1	
WALTON CLUB.CHP	4		
	82		
A.A.A CHPS.		2	1

	82	18	4

RECORDS.   TOTAL 100 CHAMPIONSHIP MEDALS

CLUB POLY 2 3 and 6 miles Record. 1HOUR 10,000 20,000 METRES

~~WALTON~~   25000 METRES and 30,000 METRES 10 miles 15 miles

5 - 7½ and 9 miles Cross Country and MARATHON,   TOTAL. 14

WALTON CLUB. 3 mile and 6 mile   2

County
IRISH 3 - 6 mile 3 and 6 mile 10000 metres 1HOUR 5 mile and 10 mile   3
                                                                        5

. WORLD Record 30,000 METRES. 1HOUR   1

1 INDOOR EUROPEAN 3 mile RECORD TOTAL   ~~25~~ 26

the distances these days because I don't really care. The best professional racing now is at the World Championships, not the Olympics. There are too many politics and vested interests involved in the Olympics.

Though I dabbled in the veterans' scene for a short while and I thought it was a good thing, I now believe that it's a total disaster for the simple reason that many people who like to coach and not compete are being lost to the vets' competitions. Many of these fellows should be putting something back into the sport rather than training themselves. I can't see any justification for fellows aged forty-five and up running a hundred miles a week. For what? Remember one thing: when you become a veteran there's only one place you're going and that's backwards. You're not going to improve, and that's a fact. I think if a lot of these older boys put a bit more back into the sport we'd be better off. We'd have a better stable if you like.

Athletics is a great sport to be in if you're good at it, but if you're not good at it, I wouldn't want to be doing it. I know fellows running a hundred miles a week and they're never going to make it. I just couldn't run a hundred miles a week and never win a race. If that kind of running wasn't improving my performance I'd go and find something else to do. I very seldom raced unless I was right. I always went for the win. I was prepared to wait for six or eight or ten weeks just to be right for a race. I would not run in a race just to make up numbers.

I have no time for people who say to me, 'Jim, you were twenty-five years too early. Look at the money you could be making today.' I have no regrets about not making money.

Sure what's money anyway? There is money in sport now and I'd say to any good athlete, 'Make what you can while you have an opportunity because it can be a very short career.' Besides, you only hear about the big earners. There are countless world-class athletes trying to live on meagre resources as professionals. I feel sorry for them because quite a few have no fallback when their career ends and they are faced with getting a job, marriage, children.

Would I do it all again? You can chalk it down, mate. If I could do it over I would go to England earlier on in my career and I might concentrate more on cultivating a better finishing drive. I never gave the mile a chance and I sometimes wonder what inroads I might have made in it. But there is no point in dwelling on any of that.

I have no regrets. A few disappointments here and there, but all things considered I didn't do too badly.

You are either born with the right musculature to be the fastest, or you are not. Excellence in sports is cruelly definitive, and that is the nausea in the pit of your stomach and in your throat, this is the fear – that you will not be good enough, and that you will be beaten, that you will fail.'

Sting. Broken Music: a Memoir. *(New York, Dial Press, 2003)*

First [the young athlete] must remember there is no short cut to the top and that it may take a long time to achieve this. He must work hard over a long period and take the rough with the smooth. Never get a big head because you are only as good as your last race and if you have a bad one this is what everyone remembers – not the good runs you had but the one bad run. So I say once again to young athletes: work hard and have faith to yourself at all times.

Jim Hogan, Athletics Weekly, *1965*